# WE DON'T
# KNOW
# EITHER

# WE DON'T KNOW EITHER

## TRIVIA NIGHT DONE RIGHT

### YOUR GUIDE TO ENTERTAINMENT, KNOWLEDGE, AND TRIVIA GAMES

mango

CORAL GABLES

Mango Publishing Group

2850 Douglas Road, 3rd Floor

Coral Gables, FL 33134 USA

info@mango.bz

For special orders, quantity sales, course adoptions and corporate sales, please email the publisher at sales@mango.bz. For trade and wholesale sales, please contact Ingram Publisher Services at customer.service@ingramcontent.com or +1.800.509.4887.

We Don't Know Either: Trivia Night Done Right

Library of Congress Cataloging

ISBN: (print) 978-1-63353-842-9 (ebook) 978-1-63353-843-6

Library of Congress Control Number: 2018952305

BISAC category code: REF018000—REFERENCE / Questions & Answers

Printed in the United States of America

# Table of Contents

HAT IS THE CAPITOL OF MARYLAND WHO INVENTEI
THE NAME WE THE ACTIOR THAT PLAYS INDIA
L DONT WROTE A MUSICALBASED ON THE LIFE OF WI
FATHER WHICH COMPANY MAKES THE IPAD EITHER
JUICE TO MAKE A SCREW DRIVER WHICH TWO NFL 1
JEW YORK HOW MANY ELEMENTS ARE ON THE PERIC
MAMBO NO 5 WHAT IS THE WESTERN MOST STA
ATES WHO WROTE THE HARRY POTTER SERIES WHAT
BACK OF THE 5 DOLLAR BILL WHAT DOES AOL STAND
MANY MEMBERS OF THE PUSSYCAT DOLLS HOW OLI
WHICH YEAR DID HENRY FORD INVENT THE MODE
INK WAS CREATED AT THE UNIVERSITY OF FLORID
AD ALL OF THESE QUESTIONS WHAT ARE YOU DOING
MANY TRIVIA WRITERS DOES IT TAKE TO CHANGE A 1
HE BOSTON MARATHON WHAT IS THE MOST VIEWEI
WHICH NETWORK HAS THE EXCLUSIVE TRIVIA TC
HOW MUCH DID A 30 SECOND NIGHT IN THE SUPER
IK IS IN THE DONE BY THE WINNER OF THE INDIANAI
IS THE GREATEST MOVIE OF ALL TIME HOW MANY EY
PLAYING CARDS WHO SHOT JR WHEN IS THE IDES
THE NAME OF THE LEADER OF NORTH KOREA WHA
RING MARCH MADNESS WHEN WAS THE CONSTITU TI
ANCH OF GOVERNMENT IS LEAD BY THE SUPREME (
KS DOES IT TAKE TO GET TO THE CENTER OF A TC
THE CITY TRIVIA HEADQUARTERS WHAT DO YOU GET
W AND BLUE WHO LIVES IN THE PINEAPPLE UNDE
THE NAME OF THE FIRST PRESIDENT OF THE UNITEI
HAT WAS THE FIRST MAND MADE OBJECT TO BREAK
HAT IS THE CAPITOL OF MARYLAND WHO INVENTEI
THE NAME WE THE ACTIOR THAT PLAYS INDIA
L DONT WROTE A MUSICALBASED ON THE LIFE OF WI

# Introduction

When we were approached about writing a trivia book our first thought was, "Sure, why not? We've already written the questions—how hard could it be?"

Then we tried to think about what the book would actually look like. Should it be a bathroom reader? Should we create something that would help someone put on their own trivia night? Should we put together a collection of party games that people can play with their friends on a Friday night? Should it be a coffee-table book that sits in your dentist's waiting room?

In true committee fashion, we decided to do all of them. So here is how you should use this book if you are...

## THE OWNER OF A BAR

Let's say you own a bar in North Dakota.

I choose North Dakota because of the North Dakota Theory. As conspiracy theories go, it is one of my favorites. You see, North Dakota does not exist. "But I've seen it on a map, it's definitely there!" Oh, you sad, naive rube. Ask yourself this... Have you ever been to North Dakota? Have you ever met anyone from North Dakota? Then how do you really know for sure that it exists?

Since it does not exist, and therefore I cannot offend anyone from there... Let's say you own a bar in North Dakota. Not many trivia companies operate in your neck of the woods, but a trivia night is one of the best things that you can do to bring in customers on a weeknight. A while ago, you tried to write the questions yourself, and it went okay for a while, but you are busy running a bar. You do not have time to worry about writing trivia questions, so you stopped asking questions and the people stopped coming.

Here is what you do: Each chapter of this book is its own trivia night. You can ask the questions for each of the five rounds for each night. I've even added in my patented sense of humor on each page. Between question rounds, we have our puzzle, picture, fill-in-the-blank, and music rounds. Just hold the book open on a copier and make as many copies as you need for the night. When your trivia night grows so big you don't have time to make copies and prep everything yourself, go to iHeartCityTrivia.com and you can order a packet that will come in the mail, ready for as many teams as you need.

## A PERSON WHO HAS NO FRIENDS

We can fix this for you. Trivia night at bars is a great place to meet new people and start making friends. Here is what you need to do: Open this book up to Chapter 1 and start memorizing questions. The more you know, the more valuable you will be to a team. You are a great person and soon will have more friends than you know what to do with. The good news is that, no matter what happens, you are improved by now having at your command a bevy of interesting facts and answers to even the most mundane of trivia questions. Unfortunately, friends are a pain in the ass. Get ready to try and coordinate your schedule with many other people, most of whom will not respond to your texts or return your phone calls. They are busy with their own stuff and they cannot be bothered to respond in a timely manner. This is how having friends works. Sometimes you will get together and have a good time, but, like I said before, most of the time you will simply be asking each other what you want to do and never coming to a consensus. Good news, though: You can now move on to the next section.

**A PERSON WHO HAS FRIENDS**

It is Saturday night and you and your friends are sitting around asking each other what you want to do tonight. You are two hours into asking that question without ever making a decision. Pull out this book, start asking questions, try to stump each other. Now you have something to do without having to make a decision. Just ask the one-pointers, and see how far you can get without getting one wrong. Ask them in order and see which difficulty is the first one you miss. Read the fill-in-the-blank round out loud and see which friend can get the most answers right. There are lots of ways to use this book sitting around on a Saturday night. Just open it up and go!

**A PERSON WHO OWNS A BUSINESS WITH A WAITING ROOM**

After years of study, schooling, and a mountain of student debt, you are now a dentist, doctor, physical therapist, ocularist (BONUS FACT: an ocularist is someone who makes glass eyes), etc. Now, your problem is, you are massively successful and have a waiting room full of people who want your services. What to do with all those people who are growing to dislike you because of how long you keep them waiting? Solution: Put this book in your waiting room. Everyone loves trivia and everyone loves knowing something that other people don't. You can now provide that to people for the very affordable cost of this book! Grab a few of these and put them on every flat surface in your waiting room. People will be so engrossed that they will forget about how long you have kept them waiting. Even better, they will share their newly learned facts with you while you examine them, so you will get smarter without ever having to read anything. After all your study, who wants to read any more?

**A PERSON WHO IS A CHARITABLE INDIVIDUAL**

You are an amazing person. The downside of hosting trivia for a living is that we don't make the big bucks. But you... You are incredible. You bought this book just to make us happy and put a few bucks in our pocket. It works great to balance a lopsided coffee table. If you buy ten of them, you can use them as a step stool. A couple of pages in this book are probably blank and you could use them to take notes on something. It doesn't matter. You're awesome. Thanks.

Regardless of how you use this book, you will have a fun time with it. We had fun writing it. No matter how you use it, enjoy!

# How to Play

### THE THREE RULES

1. No electronic devices! We want to know what you know, not what the internet tells you is true.

2. No shouting-out of answers. If you see someone doing this who isn't playing, invite them to form a team of their own if they are so smart.

3. Your host doesn't make the questions, but does make the rules. If you have an issue with a question, email contact@ iHeartCityTrivia.com, and the appropriate person will be flogged.

### TEAM SIZE

We have a very strict team size limit. Your team is allowed to have up to 35 players.

Yup, you read that right...only 35 players. Try not to go over.

### GAME PLAY

City Trivia game play consists of 5 rounds of questions with 4 bonus rounds in between. Questions are progressive and increase in difficulty and value during each round from 1 to 10 points. At the end of each round is a bonus question that uses a wager system. After hearing the question, circle the number of points you want to wager. At the end of a round, you will take that round's answer sheets to the host for scoring. You can then pick up a worksheet round to gain additional points while the host is scoring the round. Rinse and repeat.

### BONUS ROUNDS

1. Puzzle Round: Usually some sort of riddle or game that has to be worked out.

2. Picture Round: Requires you to identify ten pictures based on a theme.

3. Fill-in-the-Blank Round: Exactly what it sounds like.

4. Music Round: Identify the title and artist for ten different songs and then, as a bonus, the theme of all ten songs.

## Scoring

Question rounds: Question 1 is worth one point, Question 2 is worth two points... Get it? This means that each question round has a maximum score of 55 points.

Worksheet rounds: A perfect score on any of the worksheet rounds is usually twenty points. This means that if there are ten pictures or ten fill-in-the-blanks, then each one is worth two points.

Incorrect answers: If you have no idea of the answer to the question, then take a guess. Incorrect guesses cannot hurt you in the first ten questions of a round.

Bonus question: If you get the bonus question correct, then we add the points you wagered to your score. But, if you get the bonus question wrong, then the wager is subtracted from your score. (This is the only time when you can lose points.)

Bonus points: Hosts have the discretion of opening their magic coat of bonus points and handing them out as they see fit. For example: Making your host laugh at your stupid guesses can gain you bonus points.

Note: Since hosts can give bonus points arbitrarily, they count only for nightly scores and are not applied to tournament scores.

# How to Be a Host

Being a host is easy.

Talk out loud or on the microphone just like you would talk to a friend. Be congenial and upbeat. Everyone is there to have fun, including you. Make sure that you convey all of the needed information. Who you are, what you are doing, what the format of the game is, and remind people to have fun. That's why they are there.

Speak clearly and repeat each question. You have all of the questions and answers ahead of time. If there is a word you don't know, and we tried to provide you with phonetic pronunciation for all of them, look it up beforehand. If you make a mistake, no big deal, just laugh along with everyone else.

# How the Game Is Played

## FORMAT AND TIMING

There are nine rounds of trivia per game. Five rounds of questions and four bonus rounds of Puzzle, Picture, Fill-in-the-Blank, and Music rounds.

Once you begin asking the questions in round number one, make sure you repeat each question twice. Leave a few seconds in between each of the first few questions. They are designed to be easy and most teams will not need too much time to answer them. Questions 1–5 should take a total of about 2.5 minutes to ask. Leave thirty seconds to a minute in between questions 6–11. These questions are designed to be harder and teams will likely huddle together to debate possible answers. When you have finished, set a deadline (2 or 3 minutes) for teams to complete the round. When a team turns in the first round, give them a copy of the Puzzle round. Begin scoring the answer sheets as soon as you get them. It is up to you whether or not you accept an answer that is close, but remember, you have to deal with the consequences. Once all of the Round One answer sheets have been collected, set a deadline for the Puzzle round (again, 2–3 minutes). Ideally, you should finish scoring all of the Round One answer sheets around the time teams start turning in their Puzzle rounds. Score the Puzzle rounds as soon as you can. When you have finished scoring the Puzzle rounds, add up all of the total score of each team.

Once all Round One and Puzzle rounds have been scored and entered, read off all of the answers to Round One and the Puzzle round. Make sure to re-ask the question before giving the answer. Feel free to use any of our quips to make yourself seem funny.

After you finish reading off all of the questions and answers, review the teams' scores in order from the lowest to the highest. Repeat for Round Two and the Picture round, etc.

Each round of questions should take about 7–10 minutes to ask. You should have all answer sheets at the 13 minute mark. All puzzle rounds should be collected by 18 minutes.

You should be asking Round Two, question one, about 25 minutes after you first started Round One. A full event should run approximately 2 hours.

Every venue and every crowd is different. You, by no means, need to stick religiously to this schedule. Read the room and your players and do what makes sense.

However, remember the great proverb of Grandpa Lawrence Kaplan: "The mind can only absorb what the seat can endure." In other words, if they are sitting too long they will become *antsy* [1]

---

1 Originally this is a quote from British solicitor Donal Blaney, but my Grandpa Kaplan loved to say this. (Solicitors are what the crazy Brits call lawyers.) God Save the Queen.

# Materials

## SCRATCH PAD

The Scratch Pad Should be handed out with the answer sheets and pens. Each team should receive one. It is a place for players to record their answers for each round and allows them to follow along when you read off the answers at the end of each round. The back is also blank if the host asks them to do long division.

# TRIVIA FORMAT

5 rounds of 10 questions plus a bonus question.

Turn in answer sheets at the end of the round.

Bonus worksheets are given out at the end of Rounds 1-3. The Music Round is played at the end of Round 4.

Questions are a random mix of trivia: music, movies, sports, science, current events, literature, pop culture, and everything else!

www.iHeartCityTrivia.com

*Use this scratch pad to track your answers and scores*

# SCORING

Questions progressively increase in value and difficulty throughout each round:
1 is worth 1 point, 2 is worth 2 points, etc.

Bonus question: last question of the round. Wager how many points you want to risk.
Right answer: gain those points.
Wrong answer: lose those points.

Bonus worksheets are worth 20 points evenly divided across the questions.

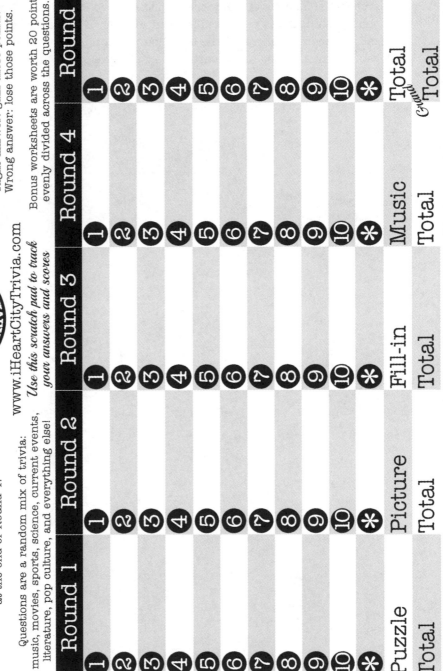

| Round 1 | Round 2 | Round 3 | Round 4 | Round 5 |
|---------|---------|---------|---------|---------|
| 1 | 1 | 1 | 1 | 1 |
| 2 | 2 | 2 | 2 | 2 |
| 3 | 3 | 3 | 3 | 3 |
| 4 | 4 | 4 | 4 | 4 |
| 5 | 5 | 5 | 5 | 5 |
| 6 | 6 | 6 | 6 | 6 |
| 7 | 7 | 7 | 7 | 7 |
| 8 | 8 | 8 | 8 | 8 |
| 9 | 9 | 9 | 9 | 9 |
| 10 | 10 | 10 | 10 | 10 |
| ✱ | ✱ | ✱ | ✱ | ✱ |
| Puzzle | Picture | Fill-in | Music | Total |
| Total | Total | Total | Total | Grand Total |

## Answer Sheet

The Answer Sheet packet should be handed out to each team in the bar. The packet should contain Rounds 1-4, the Music Round, and Round 5, in that order. 6 pages per team, stapled together. After each round of questions, teams will rip off the top sheet and turn them into the host. These are then scored and entered into the score sheet.

ROUND 1

ROUND 1

**Left card:**

1
2
3
4
5
6
7
8
9
10
✱

*Wager:* 0 1 2 3 4 5 6 7 8 9 10

*Team Name:*

ROUND SCORE

**Right card:**

1
2
3
4
5
6
7
8
9
10
✱

*Wager:* 0 1 2 3 4 5 6 7 8 9 10

*Team Name:*

ROUND SCORE

  ROUND

 ROUND **2**

1
2
3
4
5
6
7
8
9
10
✱

Wager: 0 1 2 3 4 5 6 7 8 9 10

Team
Name:

*How many players
are on your team?*

_____

1
2
3
4
5
6
7
8
9
10
✱

Wager: 0 1 2 3 4 5 6 7 8 9 10

Team
Name:

*How many players
are on your team?*

_____

  ROUND **3**

 ROUND **3**

**1**

**2**

**3**

**4**

**5**

**6**

**7**

**8**

**9**

**10**

**✳**

*Wager:* 0 1 2 3 4 5 6 7 8 9 10

*Team
Name:*

ROUND SCORE

**1**

**2**

**3**

**4**

**5**

**6**

**7**

**8**

**9**

**10**

**✳**

*Wager:* 0 1 2 3 4 5 6 7 8 9 10

*Team
Name:*

ROUND SCORE

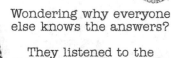

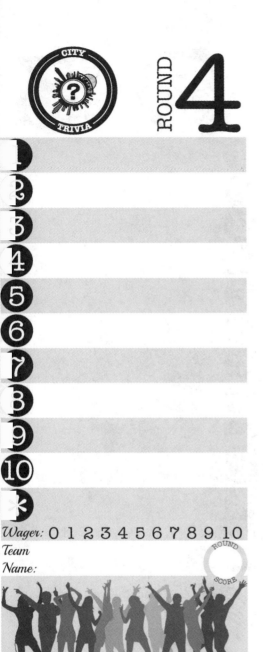

## ROUND 4

1
2
3
4
5
6
7
8
9
10
✱

Wager: 0 1 2 3 4 5 6 7 8 9 10

Team
Name:

ROUND
SCORE

Host your own Private Event!
www.iHeartCityTrivia.com

## ROUND 4

1
2
3
4
5
6
7
8
9
10
✱

Wager: 0 1 2 3 4 5 6 7 8 9 10

Team
Name:

ROUND
SCORE

Host your own Private Event!
www.iHeartCityTrivia.com

# MUSIC ROUND

*Days Like This*  *Van Morrison*

Theme: _____ (5 pts)

Team
Name: _____

Did you listen
to the podcast?

Prove it!

------------------------

www.WeDontKnowEither.com

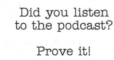 **iTunes**

# MUSIC ROUND

*Days Like This*  *Van Morrison*

Theme: _____ (5 pts)

Team
Name: _____

Did you listen
to the podcast?

Prove it!

------------------------

www.WeDontKnowEither.com

 **iTunes**

23

ROUND 5

1
2
3
4
5
6
7
8
9
10
*

Wager: 0 2 4 6 8 10 12 14 16 18 20

Team
Name:

ROUND
SCORE

*Think trivia is
fun to play?
Try hosting!*

hire.me@
iHeartCityTrivia.com

ROUND 5

1
2
3
4
5
6
7
8
9
10
*

Wager: 0 2 4 6 8 10 12 14 16 18 20

Team
Name:

ROUND
SCORE

*Think trivia is
fun to play?
Try hosting!*

hire.me@
iHeartCityTrivia.com

## Score Sheet

Fill this in with team names and scores. Better yet, recreate it in Excel and have it do the math for you.

| Team Name | R1 | PUZ | R2 | Pic | R3 | FILL | R4 | MUSIC | R5 | TOTALS |
|---|---|---|---|---|---|---|---|---|---|---|
| | | | | | | | | | | |
| | | | | | | | | | | |
| | | | | | | | | | | |
| | | | | | | | | | | |
| | | | | | | | | | | |
| | | | | | | | | | | |
| | | | | | | | | | | |
| | | | | | | | | | | |
| | | | | | | | | | | |
| | | | | | | | | | | |
| | | | | | | | | | | |
| | | | | | | | | | | |
| | | | | | | | | | | |
| | | | | | | | | | | |
| | | | | | | | | | | |

# Preface

We've asked questions about religion to a room full of priests and nuns.

We've asked NBA stars about their own accomplishments and NBA franchises about their own origins. (Both got the questions wrong.) We've asked Olympic gold medalists about their moments and Superbowl champions about football.

We've asked architects about astronomical calculations and subway employees about art.

We've stumped doctors with medical questions and unwittingly asked the head of a government agency about his own organization. Like everyone else, we've asked meteorologists about the weather.

We have asked Crayola about crayon colors and Parker Brothers about tiny metal dogs. We have stumped *Jeopardy* champions and had players spin the Wheel of Fortune. We have corrected the National Archives.

We've facilitated engagements, married couples, and...we have celebrated life. But we have yet to ask you a question.

City Trivia...what can we ask you?

# Opening Script

The opening script is how you can welcome everyone into the bar, pub, your home, or other venue for your trivia night. We have provided you a tongue in cheek example that you can use if you need one. Once you become comfortable with the main concepts, don't be afraid to change it up and add your own personal touch.

Hello and welcome to trivia night at **NAME OF VENUE** every **DAY OF WEEK** at **TIME OF EVENT.**

My name is **YOUR NAME** and I will be your host for the evening.

We have three rules that you must follow tonight.

**Rule #1:** No shouting out answers. Real or fake, don't do it. Everybody is trying to show off what they know and shouting out answers makes people unhappy. Including me...and I run the scoring. Making me unhappy is a bad idea.

**Rule #2:** No cheating. No googling answers, no phoning your friends. If you all had any friends they should be here by now. We want to know what you know, not how fast you can work your smart phone.

**Rule #3:** This is my game. That means I make the rules. I am not looking for the correct answer to the question, I am looking for the answer that is written down on my answer sheet. Luckily, those are usually one in the same.

So without further ado... Round One, Question One...

# GAME ONE

"There is much pleasure to be gained from useless knowledge."

—Bertrand Russell

HAT IS THE CAPITOL OF MARYLAND WHO INVENTE
THE NAME WE THE ACTIOR THAT PLAYS INDIA
L DONT WROTE A MUSICALBASED ON THE LIFE OF W
FATHER WHICH COMPANY MAKES THE IPAD EITHER
JUICE TO MAKE A SCREW DRIVER WHICH TWO NFL T
EW YORK HOW MANY ELEMENTS ARE ON THE PERIO
MAMBO NO 5 WHAT IS THE WESTERN MOST STA
ATES WHO WROTE THE HARRY POTTER SERIES WHAT
ACK OF THE 5 DOLLAR BILL WHAT DOES AOL STAND
MANY MEMBERS OF THE PUSSYCAT DOLLS HOW OLD
WHICH YEAR DID HENRY FORD INVENT THE MODE
INK WAS CREATED AT THE UNIVERSITY OF FLORID
AD ALL OF THESE QUESTIONS WHAT ARE YOU DOING
MANY TRIVIA WRITERS DOES IT TAKE TO CHANGE A I
HE BOSTON MARATHON WHAT IS THE MOST VIEWED
WHICH NETWORK HAS THE EXCLUSIVE TRIVIA TO
HOW MUCH DID A 30 SECOND NIGHT IN THE SUPER
K IS IN THE DONE BY THE WINNER OF THE INDIANAF
IS THE GREATEST MOVIE OF ALL TIME HOW MANY EY
PLAYING CARDS WHO SHOT JR WHEN IS THE IDES
THE NAME OF THE LEADER OF NORTH KOREA WHA
RING MARCH MADNESS WHEN WAS THE CONSTITU TI
NCH OF GOVERNMENT IS LEAD BY THE SUPREME C
S DOES IT TAKE TO GET TO THE CENTER OF A TO
HE CITY TRIVIA HEADQUARTERS WHAT DO YOU GET
W AND BLUE WHO LIVES IN THE PINEAPPLE UNDE
THE NAME OF THE FIRST PRESIDENT OF THE UNITED
HAT WAS THE FIRST MAND MADE OBJECT TO BREAK
HAT IS THE CAPITOL OF MARYLAND WHO INVENTE
THE NAME WE THE ACTIOR THAT PLAYS INDIA
L DONT WROTE A MUSICALBASED ON THE LIFE OF W

# *Round One*

1. Which common beverage is nicknamed "moo juice"?

2. Which international holiday promotes the planting of trees?

3. In which country are the D-Day beaches located?

4. Which siblings debuted as directors with the 1984 movie *Blood Simple*?

5. Which city in Thailand is nicknamed "The City of Angels"?

6. Until their falling-out in 2011, which role did New Zealander Steve Williams perform for Tiger Woods?

7. The name of which citrus fruit comes from the Cantonese for "golden orange"?

8. In which constellation does the star Aldebaran (al-deb-brr-en) mark the "red eye"?

9. In which hobby does someone use the technique "intarsia" (in-tahr-see-uh)?

10. The movies of which comedy act share names with two albums by the rock group Queen?

    **Bonus Question** Which U.S. president was the only person named *TIME* magazine's "Man of the Year" three times?

**Q8** Aldebaran is known as the Red Star. Which is funny because it is actually classified as an Orange Giant Star. This debunks the myth that the guys at NASA are smart.

**Q6** Being a caddy for
Tiger Woods in his
prime seems like an
easy job. The kind
of job that I would
be good at.

*Hey Nick, can
you hand me
that 7-iron?*

*Absolutely Tiger,
you sure you don't
want the 8?*

*Which one
of us has won
the last four
majors Nick?*

*You right Tiger,
here you go.*

Boom!

10 percent of
millions of dollars
of winnings.

# Round One
## –Answers–

1. Which common beverage is nicknamed "moo juice"?
   **Milk**

2. Which international holiday promotes the planting
   of trees? **Arbor Day**

3. In which country are the D-Day beaches located?
   **France**

4. Which siblings debuted as directors with the 1984
   movie *Blood Simple*? **Coen Brothers**

5. Which city in Thailand is nicknamed "The City of
   Angels"? **Bangkok**

6. Until their falling out in 2011, which role did New
   Zealander Steve Williams perform for Tiger Woods?
   **Caddy**

7. The name of which citrus fruit comes from the
   Cantonese name for "golden orange"? **Kumquat**

8. In which constellation does the star Aldebaran
   (al-deb-brr-en) mark the "red eye"? **Taurus**

9. In which hobby does someone use the technique
   "intarsia" (in-tahr-see-uh)? **Knitting**

10. The movies of which comedy act share names with
    two albums by the rock group Queen? **Marx Brothers**

    **Host Note** The albums are: *Day at the Races* and
    *Night at the Opera*

    **Bonus Question** Which U.S. President was the only
    person named *TIME* magazine's "Man of the Year"
    three times? **Franklin D. Roosevelt**

# Puzzle Round

Match the movie to the artist who sang its iconic song.

_____ 1. Flashdance      A. Kenny Loggins

_____ 2. The Breakfast Club      B. Stealers Wheel

_____ 3. Titanic      C. Bill Medley

_____ 4. Hercules      D. Queen

_____ 5. Reservoir Dogs      E. Michael Bolton

_____ 6. Dirty Dancing      F. Geto Boys

_____ 7. The Graduate      G. Simon & Garfunkel

_____ 8. Wayne's World      H. Celine Dion

_____ 9. Top Gun      I. Michael Sembello

_____ 10. Office Space      J. Simple Minds

**Bonus trivia question:**

Kenny Loggins sang the theme song for how many 1980s movies?

**TEAM NAME**

_____

**SCORE**

_____

# Puzzle Round
## –Answers–

Match the movie to the artist who sang its iconic song.

**Five (5)**

1. *"I'm Alright,"*
   *Caddyshack*

2. *"Footloose,"*
   *Footloose*

3. *"Meet Me Half Way,"*
   *Over the Top*

4. *"Danger Zone,"*
   *Top Gun*

5. *"Nobody's Fool,"*
   *Caddyshack II*

He is the king of
the 1980s movie
soundtrack. I
will not accept
any arguments
otherwise.

**I** 1. Flashdance     A. Kenny Loggins

**J** 2. The Breakfast Club     B. Stealers Wheel

**H** 3. Titanic     C. Bill Medley

**E** 4. Hercules     D. Queen

**B** 5. Reservoir Dogs     E. Michael Bolton

**C** 6. Dirty Dancing     F. Geto Boys

**G** 7. The Graduate     G. Simon & Garfunkel

**D** 8. Wayne's World     H. Celine Dion

**A** 9. Top Gun     I. Michael Sembello

**F** 10. Office Space     J. Simple Minds

**TEAM NAME**

_____

**SCORE**

_____

# Round Two

1. Which U.S. government body is known by the acronym "SCOTUS" (sco-tus)?

2. Which type of fruit includes the varieties plum, cherry, and beefsteak?

3. What is the phrase used to describe drinking alcohol the next morning to try to cure a hangover?

4. What is the term for the emblem on the New Orleans Saints football helmet?

5. The first two letters of which language's alphabet give us the word "alphabet"?

6. In which 2011 movie does Maya Rudolph play the bride-to-be Lillian?

7. By area, in which country is "Goa" the smallest state?

8. Which type of animal is a "coelacanth" (see-low-canth)?

9. Because of its length and position in the human body, the name of which nerve is derived from the Latin for "wandering"?

10. Before Cal Ripken, Jr. claimed the record, whose streak did Lou Gehrig break to hold the most-consecutive-games-played record in Major League Baseball?

**Bonus Question** In 2012, Kateri Tekakwitha (tech-ahh-quith-ahh) became the first Native American to be recognized as what by the Catholic church?

**Q10** I was actually at the game where Cal broke the record. It was amazing. Watching him take a victory lap, not for his own ego, but to thank the fans for being so awesome was one of the things that made me love him as a player and love the Orioles. Subsequently, that was also the last time the Orioles were any good. Go Nats!

**Q1** The Supreme Court building in Washington, D.C. has a basketball court on the fifth floor. The actual courtroom is on the second floor. This makes the basketball court the "Highest Court in the Land" that's not my joke. Actually it's not a joke at all... they actually call it that...seriously, that's what they call it. Also, I would pay lots of money to watch Ruth Bader-Ginsberg dunk on Stephen Breyer.

# Round Two
## –Answers–

1.  Which U.S. government body is known by the acronym "SCOTUS" (sco-tus)? **Supreme Court of the United States**

2.  Which type of fruit includes the varieties plum, cherry, and beefsteak? **Tomato**

3.  What is the phrase used to describe drinking alcohol the next morning to try to cure a hangover? **Hair of the Dog**

4.  What is the term for the emblem on the New Orleans Saints football helmet? **Fleur-de-lis (floor-de-lee)**

5.  The first two letters of which language's alphabet give us the word "alphabet"? **Greek**

    📝 **Host Note** Alpha + beta = alphabetos

6.  In which 2011 movie does Maya Rudolph play the bride-to-be Lillian? ***Bridesmaids***

7.  By area, in which country is "Goa" the smallest state? **India**

8.  Which type of animal is a "coelacanth" (see-low-canth)? **Fish**

9.  Because of its length and position in the human body, the name of which nerve is derived from Latin for "wandering"? **Vagus nerve**

10. Before Cal Ripken, Jr. claimed the record, whose streak did Lou Gehrig break to hold the most-consecutive-games-played record in Major League Baseball? **Everett Scott**

    📝 **Host Note** Cal Ripken, Jr.–2,632; Lou Gehrig–2,130; Everett Scott–1,307

    **Bonus Question** In 2012, Kateri Tekakwitha (tech-ahh-quith-ahh) became the first Native American to be recognized as what by the Catholic church? **Saint**

# Picture Round

Sandra Bullock: Name the Movie

1. _____

2. _____

3. _____

4. _____

5. _____

6. _____

7. _____

8. _____

9. _____

10. _____

Can we take a second to talk about the Sandra Bullock opus *The Net*? In the movie she orders a pizza from Pizza.net. In 2013 the actual domain name Pizza.net sold for about $150K. So here is my question. It's been almost thirty years since the movie… why can't I order a pizza from Pizza.net?…and don't give me any lip about the damn Domino's pizza tracker. Every time someone uses that thing it becomes one step closer to Skynet.

**TEAM NAME**

_____

**SCORE**

_____

Want more trivia?
wedontknoweither.com  dontknoweither  @wdketrivia

OK, so I have a theory about the three seashells from *Demolition Man*. I think that the first shell could be used, if you reach way around to the back...

*What? You know I really don't like it when you censor me. I don't care if you're the editor. Yes, I do want to get paid. Fine.*

Just look up "3 seashells" on Google. You'll get the idea.

**TEAM NAME**

_____

**SCORE**

_____

# Picture Round
## –Answers–

Sandra Bullock: Name the Movie

1. **Extremely Loud & Incredibly Close**

2. **Practical Magic**

3. **Speed**

4. **Miss Congeniality**

5. **Gravity**

6. **The Blind Side**

7. **All About Steve**

8. **The Heat**

9. **A Time to Kill**

10. **Demolition Man**

Want more trivia?
wedontknoweither.com  **f** 🐦 *dontknoweither* 📷 *@wdketrivia*

# Round Three

1.  What number is represented by a one followed by six zeroes?

2.  In which city do both the Lakers and Clippers NBA teams play their home games?

3.  Which part of the human body is commonly known as the "voice box"?

4.  Which group of islands is abbreviated as "BVI"?

5.  In which town did Superman grow up?

6.  In 1985, which shipwreck was found by explorer Robert Ballard?

7.  In the iconic 1993 "Nothing but Net" McDonald's commercial, who played a game of horse with Michael Jordan?

8.  In the comic strip *Ziggy*, what is the name of Ziggy's dog?

9.  A doctor of which medical specialty typically uses a "ventouse" (vahn-toos)?

10. Before it was covered by Bananarama, which 1970s band originally performed the song "Venus"?

**Bonus Question** Created for the 1972 Munich Olympic Games, which breed of dog was Waldi, the first official Olympic mascot?

**Q1** The largest number with a name, generally accepted in the U.S. in mathematics, is not a googolplex. What you learned in kindergarten was not correct. Shocking, I know. The number is actually a Centillion. Which is a 1 followed by 303 zeros.

*Why 303 zeros?*

Because math people hate everyone.

**Bonus** Considering what the mascots of the Olympics are now, a dog seems downright pedestrian. Officially and unofficially, we have had a

• blue tear-shaped blob,

• anthropomorphic representations of participation and equality,

• and Fatso the Fat-Arsed Wombat.

I liked Fatso. He was relatable.

# Round Three
## –Answers–

1. What number is represented by a one followed by six zeroes? **One million**

2. In which city do both the Lakers and Clippers NBA teams play their home games? **Los Angeles**

3. Which part of the human body is commonly known as the "voice box"? **Larynx**

4. Which group of islands is abbreviated as "BVI"? **British Virgin Islands**

5. In which town did Superman grow up? **Smallville**

6. In 1985, which shipwreck was found by explorer Robert Ballard? *Titanic*

7. In the iconic 1993 "Nothing but Net" McDonald's commercial, who played a game of horse with Michael Jordan? **Larry Bird**

8. In the comic strip *Ziggy*, what is the name of Ziggy's dog? **Fuzz**

9. A doctor of which medical specialty typically uses a "ventouse" (vahn-toos)? **Obstetrician**

   ✎ **Host Note** A ventouse is a vacuum device used to help deliver a child. It is also used by midwives.

10. Before it was covered by Bananarama, which 1970s band originally performed the song "Venus"? **Shocking Blue**

    **Bonus Question** Created for the 1972 Munich Olympic Games, which breed of dog was Waldi, the first official Olympic mascot? **Dachshund** (dox-hund)

# Fill-in-the-Blank Round

Fill-in the bordering country that begins
with the same letter.

1. Iran _____

2. Bolivia _____

3. Zambia _____

4. Latvia _____

5. Kyrgyzstan _____

6. Armenia _____

7. Ethiopia _____

8. Central African Republic _____

9. Burkina Faso _____

10. Mozambique _____

Geography is a tough trivia topic. Not only are there too many countries in the world, but they keep changing all the time. Depending on when you are reading this book, most of these countries may not even exist anymore.

If it is way in the future and this book is in a museum of Pop Culture of the early 2000s, please do not use historical records of my Facebook account to come to any conclusions about me.

I am really not THAT into cats.

**TEAM NAME**

_____

**SCORE**

_____

Who is in charge of
naming countries?
I really feel like
most of them come
about because
people got sick of
referring to, "That
place over there
with the people
who are different
from us." I would
call my country
"Schlunderplin."

*Why would you
call it that?*

Why indeed,
dear reader,
why indeed.

**TEAM NAME**

_____

**SCORE**

_____

# Fill-in-the-Blank Round
## –Answers–

Fill-in the bordering country that begins
with the same letter.

1. Iran **Iraq**

2. Bolivia **Brazil**

3. Zambia **Zimbabwe**

4. Latvia **Lithuania**

5. Kyrgyzstan **Kazakhstan**

6. Armenia **Azerbaijan**

7. Ethiopia **Eritrea**

8. Central African Republic **Chad**

9. Burkina Faso **Benin**

10. Mozambique **Malawi**

# Round Four

1. Which type of animal is commonly called a "chimp"?

2. Which phrase was used to refer to the rivalry between the U.S.A. and U.S.S.R. to reach the Moon?

3. As of 2018, how many rounds are in the NFL (National Football League) draft?

4. According to the first line of the novel *Gone with the Wind*, who was "not beautiful"?

5. After a fifty-four-year absence, which sledding event returned to the Winter Olympics in 2002?

6. Which Broadway musical is about the last seven days in the life of Jesus?

7. In the novel *The Hobbit*, what was the name of Bilbo Baggins' house?

8. As of 2018, how many wide receivers have won the Heisman Trophy?

9. From which mountain range does the St. Bernard dog derive its name?

10. Which actress is formally addressed as Lady Haden-Guest?

**Bonus Question** In 1988, which item of clothing appeared for the first time on the cover of *Vogue*?

**Q3** Back in 1992, the draft was twelve rounds long. In 1993 they lowered it to eight. Can you imagine being the guy who would have been picked with the first pick of the ninth round in 1993? You just got screwed out of a career playing in the NFL. All that work for nothing because some billionaire owner somewhere didn't feel like sitting around a posh New York hotel for another few hours.

**Q10** Christopher Guest is a Baron??? That definitely isn't right. He will forever be a Count

...and have six fingers

...and have killed my father

...he should prepare to die.

# Round Four
## -Answers-

1. Which type of animal is commonly called a "chimp"?
   **Chimpanzee**

2. Which phrase was used to refer to the rivalry between the U.S.A. and U.S.S.R. to reach the Moon?
   **Space race**

3. As of 2018, how many rounds are in the NFL (National Football League) draft? **Seven (7)**

4. According to the first line of the novel *Gone with the Wind*, who was "not beautiful"? **Scarlett O'Hara**

5. After a fifty-four-year absence, which sledding event returned to the Winter Olympics in 2002? **Skeleton**

6. Which Broadway musical is about the last seven days in the life of Jesus? *Jesus Christ Superstar*

7. In the novel *The Hobbit*, what was the name of Bilbo Baggins' house? **Bag End**

8. As of 2018, how many wide receivers have won the Heisman Trophy? **Three (3)**

   **Host Note** Johnny Rogers in 1972, Tim Brown in 1987, and Desmond Howard in 1991.

9. From which mountain range does the St. Bernard dog derive its name? **The Alps**

10. Which actress is formally addressed as Lady Haden-Guest? **Jamie Lee Curtis**

    **Host Note** She is married to Christopher Guest, the Baron Haden-Guest.

    **Bonus Question** In 1988, which item of clothing appeared for the first time on the cover of *Vogue*?
    **Jeans**

# Music Round

Name the song and the artist/band.

1. Oh, where oh where can my baby be? /
   The Lord took her away from me

   _____ by _____

2. There used to be a graying tower alone on the sea /
   You became the light on the dark side of me

   _____ by _____

3. Don't need to wait for an invitation /
   You gotta live like you're on vacation

   _____ by _____

4. Look at me can't you see / All I really want to be

   _____ by _____

5. Everybody riding shotgun, scared to play the driver /
   Ci, got the pedal to the medal going super light-speed

   _____ by _____

6. No, I don't even know your name / It doesn't matter
   / You're my experimental game / Just human nature

   _____ by _____

7. Dressing like your sister / Living like a tart / They
   don't know what you're doing / Babe, it must be art

   _____ by _____

8. You think maybe I need help, no, I know that I'm right
   / I'm just better off not listening to friends' advice

   _____ by _____

9. All that I've been given / Is this pain that I've been
   living / They got me in the system / Why they gotta
   do me like that?

   _____ by _____

10. Lift your open hand / Strike up the band, and make
    the fireflies dance silver moon's sparkling

    _____ by _____

Theme

_____

Poetry is lyrics
without music. Lyrics
without music is like
a body without a
soul. I have no idea
what that means, but
it sounds deep

…also, I hate poetry.

CITY TRIVIA

**TEAM NAME**

_____

**SCORE**

_____

# Music Round
## -Answers-

Name the song and the artist/band.

1. Oh, where oh where can my baby be? / The Lord took her away from me **Last Kiss** by **Pearl Jam**

2. There used to be a graying tower alone on the sea / You became the light on the dark side of me **Kiss From a Rose** by **Seal**

3. Don't need to wait for an invitation / You gotta live like you're on vacation **Lick It Up** by **KISS**

4. Look at me can't you see / All I really want to be **Suck My Kiss** by **Red Hot Chili Peppers**

5. Everybody riding shotgun, scared to play the driver / Ci, got the pedal to the medal going super light-speed **Pucker Up** by **Ciara**

6. No, I don't even know your name / It doesn't matter / You're my experimental game / Just human nature **I Kissed a Girl** by **Katy Perry**

7. Dressing like your sister / Living like a tart / They don't know what you're doing / Babe, it must be art **Hold Me, Thrill Me, Kiss Me, Kill Me** by **U2**

8. You think maybe I need help, no, I know that I'm right / I'm just better off not listening to friends' advice **Kiss On My List** by **Hall & Oates**

9. All that I've been given / Is this pain that I've been living / They got me in the system / Why they gotta do me like that? **Why** by **Jadakiss**

10. Lift your open hand / Strike up the band, and make the fireflies dance silver moon's sparkling **Kiss Me** by **Sixpence None the Richer**

    Theme: **Kissing**

**TEAM NAME**

**SCORE**

# Round Five

1.  In which city did the Wizard of Oz live?

2.  Which type of long, narrow skirt is named after a writing utensil?

3.  In the acronym "ETA," what does the "E" stand for?

4.  Who played the title role in both of the movies *Taxi Driver* and *Raging Bull*?

5.  Of which South American country is Caracas (kah-rock-us) the capital city?

6.  Which actress has the coordinates of her children's birthplaces tattooed on her arm?

7.  What is the term used for the volume of whiskey lost as it matures in the barrel?

8.  Which 1988 movie reimagines a famous scientist as a farmer who discovers rock 'n' roll?

9.  In which modern-day country was tennis player Novak Djokovic (joe-ko-vic) born?

10. What word for "crazy" is a descriptor for clowns in the Italian theater?

**Bonus Question** Who was the first person to share the cover of *O* magazine with Oprah Winfrey?

**Q5** Here's your piece of trivia advice for this round from the expert. Memorize your South American countries and capitals. There are only twelve countries. It's easy. One-seventh of all trivia geography questions are about South America. Just take twenty minutes and do it

...also, 72.643 percent of statistics are made up.

**Q7** The "Angel's Share" is lost mainly due to evaporation. The new cool term that has been recently added to the whiskey scene is "Devil's Cut," which is reclaimed by pressing the wooden stave's of the barrel and squeezing out some of the fluid that has been absorbed... A stave is a plank that you use to make a barrel...a barrel is a cylindrical container that refers to a quantity of forty-three U.S. gallons

...that's all I got

...IS THAT NOT ENOUGH FOR YOU???

# Round Five
## –Answers–

1. In which city did the Wizard of Oz live? **Emerald City**

2. Which type of long, narrow skirt is named after a writing utensil? **Pencil skirt**

3. In the acronym "ETA," what does the "E" stand for? **Estimated**

4. Who played the title role in both of the movies *Taxi Driver* and *Raging Bull*? **Robert DeNiro**

5. Of which South American country is Caracas (kah-rock-us) the capital city? **Venezuela**

6. Which actress has the coordinates of her children's birthplaces tattooed on her arm? **Angelina Jolie**

7. What is the term used for the volume of whiskey lost as it matures in the barrel? **The angels' share**

   **Host Note** About 2 percent is lost, depending on the climate.

8. Which 1988 movie reimagines a famous scientist as a farmer who discovers rock 'n' roll? ***Young Einstein***

9. In which modern day country was tennis player Novak Djokovic (joe-ko-vic) born? **Serbia**

   **Host Note** When Novak was born, the country was Yugoslavia.

10. What word for "crazy" is a descriptor for clowns in the Italian theater? **Zany**

    **Bonus Question** Who was the first person to share the cover of *O* magazine with Oprah Winfrey? **Michelle Obama**

    **Host Note** On the April 2009 issue.

# GAME TWO

"If you think education is expensive, try ignorance."

—Derek Bok

HAT IS THE CAPITOL OF MARYLAND WHO INVENTE
THE NAME WE THE ACTIOR THAT PLAYS INDIA
L DONT WROTE A MUSICALBASED ON THE LIFE OF W
FATHER WHICH COMPANY MAKES THE IPAD EITHER
JUICE TO MAKE A SCREW DRIVER WHICH TWO NFL
EW YORK HOW MANY ELEMENTS ARE ON THE PERIO
MAMBO NO 5 WHAT IS THE WESTERN MOST STA
ATES WHO WROTE THE HARRY POTTER SERIES WHA
BACK OF THE 5 DOLLAR BILL WHAT DOES AOL STAND
MANY MEMBERS OF THE PUSSYCAT DOLLS HOW OL
WHICH YEAR DID HENRY FORD INVENT THE MODE
INK WAS CREATED AT THE UNIVERSITY OF FLORID
AD ALL OF THESE QUESTIONS WHAT ARE YOU DOING
MANY TRIVIA WRITERS DOES IT TAKE TO CHANGE A
HE BOSTON MARATHON WHAT IS THE MOST VIEWEL
WHICH NETWORK HAS THE EXCLUSIVE TRIVIA TC
HOW MUCH DID A 30 SECOND NIGHT IN THE SUPER
K IS IN THE DONE BY THE WINNER OF THE INDIANAF
IS THE GREATEST MOVIE OF ALL TIME HOW MANY EY
PLAYING CARDS WHO SHOT JR WHEN IS THE IDES
THE NAME OF THE LEADER OF NORTH KOREA WHA
RING MARCH MADNESS WHEN WAS THE CONSTITU TI
ANCH OF GOVERNMENT IS LEAD BY THE SUPREME C
S DOES IT TAKE TO GET TO THE CENTER OF A TC
HE CITY TRIVIA HEADQUARTERS WHAT DO YOU GET
W AND BLUE WHO LIVES IN THE PINEAPPLE UNDE
THE NAME OF THE FIRST PRESIDENT OF THE UNITED
HAT WAS THE FIRST MAND MADE OBJECT TO BREAK
HAT IS THE CAPITOL OF MARYLAND WHO INVENTE
THE NAME WE THE ACTIOR THAT PLAYS INDIA
L DONT WROTE A MUSICALBASED ON THE LIFE OF W

# Round One

1. What is the largest single-digit number?

2. Which unit of measurement is abbreviated "yd"?

3. What is the term for the medical procedure in which blood is transferred intravenously into the circulatory system?

4. In poker, what is the term for a hand containing any five cards of the same suit?

5. In ten-pin bowling, how many strikes are needed to score a 300?

6. Which Italian red wine shares its name with a Tuscan mountain range?

7. Which Shakespearean play includes the line "This above all: to thine own self be true"?

8. Named after the physician Willian H. Bates, what is improved by using the Bates Method?

9. Which fruit shares its name with an organ found in the heads of whales and dolphins?

10. In 1993, which British actor opened a center for helping children who stutter?

   **Bonus Question** Which is the only U.S. state that can be typed using only one row of keys on a QWERTY keyboard?

**Q9** In dolphins, the melon is a deposit of fatty tissue in its forehead. It uses it for echolocation. What does your fatty deposit do?

# *Round One*
## –Answers–

1. What is the largest single-digit number? **Nine (9)**

2. Which unit of measurement is abbreviated "yd"? **Yard**

3. What is the term for the medical procedure where blood is transferred intravenously into the circulatory system? **Transfusion**

4. In poker, what is the term for a hand containing any five cards of the same suit? **Flush**

5. In ten-pin bowling, how many strikes are needed to score a 300? **Twelve (12)**

6. Which Italian red wine shares its name with a Tuscan mountain range? **Chianti (key-an-tea)**

7. Which Shakespearean play includes the line "This above all: to thine own self be true"? ***Hamlet***

8. Named after the physician Willian H. Bates, what is improved by using the Bates Method? **Eyesight**

9. Which fruit shares its name with an organ found in the heads of whales and dolphins? **Melon**

10. In 1993, which British actor opened a center for helping children who stutter? **Michael Palin**

    **Bonus Question** Which is the only U.S. state that can be typed using only one row of keys on a QWERTY keyboard? **Alaska**

# Puzzle Round

Match the famous person to their first words.

_____ 1. George Orwell      A. Up

_____ 2. Pablo Picasso      B. Home

_____ 3. Bill Clinton      C. ¡Ay Caramba!

_____ 4. Neil Young      D. Don't do that!

_____ 5. Julie Andrews      E. Beastly

_____ 6. Scott Fitzgerald      F. Why

_____ 7. Steven Spielberg      G. Piz

_____ 8. Bart Simpson      H. Papa

_____ 9. Amelia Earhart      I. Pappaw

_____ 10. Russell Brand      J. Dombeen

I have a son. One of my proudest moments as a father was when his first word was "daddy." That lasted for about a week, when I became even prouder at his second words. "Not Daddy." That's what he called my wife for almost two months. She was less than amused.

**TEAM NAME**

_____

**SCORE**

_____

Steven Spielberg's first word was "Why?" I do not envy his parents. Toddlers ask enough questions without them starting the moment they begin speaking. I guess he made up for it after the fact. I hope my kid buys me a million-dollar house one day.

# Puzzle Round
## –Answers–

Match the famous person to their first words.

| | | |
|---|---|---|
| **E** 1. George Orwell | A. Up |
| **G** 2. Pablo Picasso | B. Home |
| **I** 3. Bill Clinton | C. ¡Ay Caramba! |
| **J** 4. Neil Young | D. Don't do that! |
| **B** 5. Julie Andrews | E. Beastly |
| **A** 6. Scott Fitzgerald | F. Why |
| **F** 7. Steven Spielberg | G. Piz |
| **C** 8. Bart Simpson | H. Papa |
| **H** 9. Amelia Earhart | I. Pappaw |
| **D** 10. Russell Brand | J. Dombeen |

**TEAM NAME**

**SCORE**

# Round Two

1. What makes up a "motorcade"?

2. Which star is closest to the planet Mercury?

3. How many Horsemen of the Apocalypse are in the King James Bible?

4. Which type of bee mates with the queen?

5. In 2001, which word was removed from the name of MLB's (Major League Baseball) Tampa Bay franchise?

6. In which cartoon series do the words "30th Century Fox" appear in the end credits?

7. In the movie *Beverly Hills Cop*, for which police department does Axel Foley work as a detective?

8. What is the term for an official document issued by the Pope?

9. Which 2010 movie is based on the book *The Accidental Billionaires* by Ben Mezrich?

10. As of 2018, how many NHL (National Hockey League) teams have never won the Stanley Cup?

   **Bonus Question** In 2012, which actor became the first male face of Chanel No. 5?

**Q3** Umm...let's see... Horsemen of the Apocalypse...there was Pestilence, Famine... Carrot Top, Dick Cheney, the guy who made *The Room*, and...Betty White? I remember something about White.

**Q4** So a drone's only responsibility is to mate with the queen. I know this sounds like my dream job, but thinking about it just makes me tired. Nothing but mating all day? With a fertile queen. Who wants offspring. Think about that. That's your only job. What if you're bad at it? What if she talks to her friends about you? Uh-uh... hard pass.

# Round Two
## -Answers-

1. What makes up a "motorcade"? **Motorized vehicles**

2. Which star is closest to the planet Mercury? **Sun (Sol)**

3. How many Horsemen of the Apocalypse are in the King James Bible? **Four (4)**

4. Which type of bee mates with the queen? **Drone**

5. In 2001, which word was removed from the name of MLB's Tampa Bay franchise? **Devil**

   🖊 **Host Note** It was changed to just Rays.

6. In which cartoon series do the words "30th Century Fox" appear in the end credits? ***Futurama***

7. In the movie *Beverly Hills Cop*, for which police department does Axel Foley work as a detective? **Detroit, Michigan**

8. What is the term for an official document issued by the Pope? **Papal bull**

9. Which 2010 movie is based on the book *The Accidental Billionaires* by Ben Mezrich? ***The Social Network***

10. As of 2018, how many NHL (National Hockey League) teams have never won the Stanley Cup? **Thirteen (13)**

    **Bonus Question** In 2012, which actor became the first male face of Chanel No. 5? **Brad Pitt**

# Picture Round

## Famous Spokesperson: Name the Company

1. _____

2. _____

3. _____

4. _____

5. _____

6. _____

7. _____

8. _____

9. _____

10. _____

Ok here is the deal. I need to be famous enough for someone to hire me on as a celebrity spokesman. In order to do that, we need to work together to sell a couple of million copies of this book. It doesn't really matter to me if that's two million people buying one book or one person buying two million books. So Bill Gates, if you are reading this...please?

**TEAM NAME**

_____

**SCORE**

_____

Yes, we know that Jonathan Goldsmith retired as The Most Interesting Man in the World and is no longer the spokesman for Dos Equis. We also know that he is now the spokesman for a brand of Tequila. Point is, print books don't change. Just name the company in the picture and stop complaining... and yes, I did hear you complain. I have good ears.

**TEAM NAME**

_____

**SCORE**

_____

# Picture Round
## –Answers–

Famous Spokesperson: Name the Company

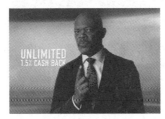

1. **Capital One**
(Samuel L. Jackson)

2. **Sonic**
(T.J. Jagodowshski)

4. **E-Trade**
(Kevin Spacy)

4. **Wendy's**
(Morgan Smith)

5. **Lincoln**
(Matthew McConaughey)

6. **At&T**
(Milana Vayntrub)

7. **Hotels.com**
(Brandon Moynihan)

8. **Progressive**
(Stephanie Courtney)

9. **Hotels.com**
(William Shatner)

10. **Dos Equis**
(Jonathan Goldsmith)

Want more trivia?
wedontknoweither.com

 *dontknoweither* @wdktrivia

# Round Three

1. Which horse won the Triple Crown of Thoroughbred Racing in 2018?

2. For which number is "twain" an old term?

3. For the movie *American Pie*, which type of fruit was in the pie featured on the movie poster?

4. Which car company makes the Fusion?

5. What is the name of the period in U.S. history when alcohol was illegal?

6. As of 2018, who holds the men's record for most titles at a single Grand Slam tennis tournament?

7. In which country was scientist Marie Curie born?

8. Named after a U.S. President, what was the term used for the shanty towns that appeared throughout the United States during the Great Depression?

9. In which body of water are the Dodecanese (doh-dek-uh-nees) Islands located?

10. In the *X-Men* comics, which substance is used to contain the optic blasts of Cyclops?

**Bonus Question** As of the 2018 Winter Olympics, which country has won the most medals at the Winter Olympics?

**Q1** Did you know that all of the horses that race in the triple crown are three years old. Can you imagine peaking at three? Sorry guy, you were at the top of your game at three, but ever since then it's been downhill. You really struggled with the potty training and your finger painting is atrocious. Better shape up soon or we are going to have to turn you into glue.

**Q5** Prohibition is one of those periods of American history that is fascinating. For example, contrary to popular belief, it was not illegal to DRINK alcohol during prohibition. It was only illegal to produce, sell, or transport alcohol intended for consumption. This led to the rise of dive bars called "Blind Pigs." A place where customers would pay to see an attraction, like a petting-zoo pig, and receive a free drink. America, king of the workaround.

# Round Three
## –Answers–

1. Which horse won the Triple Crown of Thoroughbred Racing in 2018? **Justify**

2. For which number is "twain" an old term? **Two (2)**

3. For the movie *American Pie*, which type of fruit was in the pie featured on the movie poster? **Apple**

4. Which car company makes the Fusion? **Ford**

5. What is the name of the period in U.S. history when alcohol was illegal? **Prohibition**

6. As of 2018, who holds the men's record for most titles at a single Grand Slam tennis tournament? **Rafael Nadal**

    **Host Note** A total of ten at the French Open.

7. In which country was scientist Marie Curie born? **Poland (Warsaw)**

8. Named after a U.S. President, what was the term used for the shanty towns that appeared throughout the United States during the Great Depression? **Hoovervilles**

9. In which body of water are the Dodecanese (doh-dek-uh-nees) Islands located? **Aegean (a-gee-ann) Sea**

10. In the *X-Men* comics, which substance is used to contain the optic blasts of Cyclops? **Ruby quartz**

    **Bonus Question** As of the 2018 Winter Olympics, which country has won the most medals at the Winter Olympics? **Norway**

# Fill-in-the-Blank Round

Fill-in the company that makes the toy product.

1. Xbox One _____

2. Barbie _____

3. Mindstorms _____

4. Mario Bros. _____

5. Furby _____

6. Frisbee _____

7. Power Wheels _____

8. Monopoly _____

9. LeapPad _____

10. Bratz _____

Can we talk about the evolution of toys and childhood in this country? The fact that we have gone from a Frisbee to an Xbox One in about one hundred years is astounding. Seriously, try and get a kid of today to play with a ball and cup. They will look at you like you're an idiot. Come to think of it, I would bet a kid from the early 1900s would look at you like you were an idiot too. The ball and cup sucks as a toy.

**TEAM NAME**

_____

**SCORE**

_____

I bought my son a LeapPad. I thought it would be a fun way to introduce him to tablets while playing age-appropriate games. It lasted for about five minutes before he grabbed my iPad and started using that. Way to provide a product that fills a five-minute window LeapFrog.

# Fill-in-the-Blank Round
## –Answers–

Fill-in the company that makes the toy product.

1. Xbox One **Microsoft**

2. Barbie **Mattel**

3. Mindstorms **Lego**

4. Mario Bros. **Nintendo**

5. Furby **Tiger Electronics or Hasbro**

6. Frisbee **Wham-o**

7. Power Wheels **Fisher Price**

8. Monopoly **Hasbro or Parker Brothers**

9. LeapPad **LeapFrog**

10. Bratz **MGA Entertainment**

# Round Four

1. In the classic party game, what do children pin on a donkey?

2. Which style of hat is worn by Speedy Gonzales?

3. In geology, what can be extinct, dormant, active, or erupting?

4. Which muscle of the upper arm has a name meaning "three heads"?

5. In which language does "hot" translate to *"caliente"* (cah-lee-en-tay)?

6. In a P2P computer network, what does "P2P" stand for?

7. As of 2018, which player holds the record for most selections to the NBA All-Star Game?

8. What does an anthropophagous (an-throw-po-fay-gus) person eat?

9. What is the term for the froth or foam on the sea?

10. What is "amychophobia" (a-mee-cho-foh-bee-uh) the fear of?

**Bonus Question** According to Urban Dictionary, which date is recognized as "National Hangover Day"?

**Q2** Speedy Gonzalez has a cousin named Slowpoke Gonzalez. He was created as a stereotype of Mexican culture. In fact, if you look back at a lot of the old cartoons you can see that the racism of the...*what's that?... keep it upbeat and light?...don't delve into the treacherous waters of social commentary?* This is the issue with editors, reader, they are more concerned with not offending people than actual cool facts. But since they write the checks...go America!

**Q1** Pin the Tail on the Donkey is believed to have begun in the late 1880s. It was so popular that people began throwing Donkey Parties. They were vastly different than the Donkey Parties of modern day Tijuana.

# Round Four
## –Answers–

1. In the classic party game, what do children pin on a donkey? **Tail**

2. Which style of hat is worn by Speedy Gonzales? **Sombrero**

3. In geology, what can be extinct, dormant, active, or erupting? **Volcanoes**

4. Which muscle of the upper arm has a name meaning "three heads"? **Triceps**

5. In which language does "hot" translate to *"caliente"* (cah-lee-en-tay)? **Spanish**

6. In a P2P computer network, what does "P2P" stand for? **Peer to peer**

7. As of 2018, which player holds the record for most selections to the NBA All-Star Game? **Kareem Abdul-Jabbar**

   **Host Note** He has nineteen. Kobe Bryant is second with eighteen.

8. What does an anthropophagous (an-throw-po-fay-gus) person eat? **Human flesh**

9. What is the term for the froth or foam on the sea? **Spume (spyoom)**

10. What is "amychophobia" (a-mee-cho-foh-bee-uh) the fear of? **Being scratched or clawed**

    **Bonus Question** According to Urban Dictionary, which date is recognized as "National Hangover Day"? **January 1**

# Music Round

Name the song and the artist/band.

1. She hid around corners and she hid under beds /
   She killed it with kisses and from it she fled

   _____ by _____

2. She said "I'm fine, I'm okay" cover up your
   trembling hands / There's indecision when you know
   you ain't got nothing left

   _____ by _____

3. Desert loving in your eyes all the way / If I listen to
   your lies, would you say

   _____ by _____

4. I'm just another heart in need of rescue, / Waiting
   on love's sweet charity

   _____ by _____

5. Woman you want me give me a sign / And catch my
   breathing even closer behind

   _____ by _____

6. Finally, someone let me out of my cage / Now time
   for me is nothing 'cause I'm counting no age

   _____ by _____

7. He was a hard-headed man he was brutally
   handsome / And she was terminally pretty

   _____ by _____

8. So this ain't the end, I saw you again today / Had to
   turn my heart away

   _____ by _____

9. Well, my baby and me went out late Saturday
   night / I had my hair piled high and my baby just
   looked so right

   _____ by _____

10. Love, the kind you clean up with a mop and bucket
    / Like the lost catacombs of Egypt

    _____ by _____

Theme _____

It always amazes me how hard song lyrics are to guess without the music. I am terrible at music rounds on trivia nights. I sing along word-for-word to every song that is played and when I can't pull the title OR the artist, my friends hate me. Upon reflection, their hating me may have more to do with my personality than my lack of music knowledge.

**TEAM NAME**

_____

**SCORE**

_____

Songfact.com lists over 600 songs with animals in the title. Throw in bands with animals in their name and that number easily goes over 1,000. Statistics like this always makes me wonder what the number one theme is for songs and band names. I'm guessing women's names.

What is your guess? Tweet us @CityTrivia to let us know what you think.

# *Music Round*
## –Answers–
Name the song and the artist/band.

1. She hid around corners and she hid under beds / She killed it with kisses and from it she fled
**Dog Days Are Over** by **Florence + the Machine**

2. She said "I'm fine, I'm okay" cover up your trembling hands / There's indecision when you know you ain't got nothing left
**Fall Down** by **Toad the Wet Sprocket**

3. Desert loving in your eyes all the way / If I listen to your lies, would you say
**Karma Chameleon** by **Culture Club**

4. I'm just another heart in need of rescue, / Waiting on love's sweet charity
**Here I Go Again** by **Whitesnake**

5. Woman you want me give me a sign / And catch my breathing even closer behind
**Hungry Like the Wolf** by **Duran Duran**

6. Finally, someone let me out of my cage / Now time for me is nothing 'cause I'm counting no age
**Clint Eastwood** by **Gorillaz**

7. He was a hard-headed man he was brutally handsome / And she was terminally pretty
**Life in the Fast Lane** by **The Eagles**

8. So this ain't the end, I saw you again today / Had to turn my heart away **Barracuda** by **Heart**

9. Well, my baby and me went out late Saturday night / I had my hair piled high and my baby just looked so right **Rock This Town** by **Stray Cats**

10. Love, the kind you clean up with a mop and bucket / Like the lost catacombs of Egypt **The Bad Touch** by **Bloodhound Gang**

Theme: **Animals**

# Round Five

1. If something is trisected, into how many parts is it divided?

2. In astronomy, which term means "between stars"?

3. In which sport was the founder of French clothing company Lacoste a champion?

4. Which major river runs through Cairo, Egypt?

5. What is the traditional color of the liqueur "creme de menthe"?

6. Which David Bowie song opens with the lyric "Ground Control to Major Tom"?

7. The name of which egg-based dish is derived from the French word for "to blow or puff up"?

8. As of 2018, which university was the lowest-seeded team to win an NCAA Men's Basketball Tournament?

9. In which country is the Tirari (teh-raw-ree) Desert?

10. Who was the first author to have an autobiography listed in Oprah's Book Club?

**Bonus Question** As of November 2017, according to the TOP500 project rankings, in which country is the world's fastest supercomputer located?

**Q2** Scientists at CERN have found a way to make particles move faster than the speed of light. How is no one talking about this? Also, on an unimportant note, time to rewrite all of our "fastest something can move" questions. I hate science.

**Q1** Trivia Night Tip: Much like the SATs, you would do well to commit Latin root word origins to memory. Especially in regards to numbers. Bi is two, tri is three. I won't go into all of them, but the most interesting one is zero, nulli.

# Round Five
## –Answers–

1. If something is trisected, into how many parts is it divided? **Three (3)**

2. In astronomy, which term means "between stars"? **Interstellar**

3. In which sport was the founder of French clothing company Lacoste a champion? **Tennis**

   🖊 **Host Note** The founder was René Lacoste.

4. Which major river runs through Cairo, Egypt? **Nile**

5. What is the traditional color of the liqueur "creme de menthe"? **Green**

   🖊 **Host Note** It is also available colorless.

6. Which David Bowie song opens with the lyric "Ground Control to Major Tom"? **Space Oddity**

7. The name of which egg-based dish is derived from the French word for "to blow or puff up"? **Soufflé (soo-flay)**

8. As of 2018, which university was the lowest-seeded team to win an NCAA Men's Basketball Tournament? **Villanova**

   🖊 **Host Note** The number eight seed in 1985.

9. In which country is the Tirari (teh-raw-ree) Desert? **Australia**

10. Who was the first author to have an autobiography listed in Oprah's Book Club? **Maya Angelou (May 1997)**

    **Bonus Question** As of November 2017, according to the TOP500 project rankings, in which country is the world's fastest supercomputer located? **China**

    🖊 **Host Note** The computer is the Sunway TaihuLight.

# GAME THREE

"Every man is a fool for at least five minutes every day;
wisdom comes in not exceeding the limit."

—Elbert Hubbard

HAT IS THE CAPITOL OF MARYLAND WHO INVENTED
THE NAME WE THE ACTIOR THAT PLAYS INDIA
L DONT WROTE A MUSICALBASED ON THE LIFE OF WI
FATHER WHICH COMPANY MAKES THE IPAD EITHER
JUICE TO MAKE A SCREW DRIVER WHICH TWO NFL T
EW YORK HOW MANY ELEMENTS ARE ON THE PERIO
MAMBO NO 5 WHAT IS THE WESTERN MOST STA
ATES WHO WROTE THE HARRY POTTER SERIES WHAT
ACK OF THE 5 DOLLAR BILL WHAT DOES AOL STAND
ANY MEMBERS OF THE PUSSYCAT DOLLS HOW OLL
WHICH YEAR DID HENRY FORD INVENT THE MODE
INK WAS CREATED AT THE UNIVERSITY OF FLORID
AD ALL OF THESE QUESTIONS WHAT ARE YOU DOING
ANY TRIVIA WRITERS DOES IT TAKE TO CHANGE A I
HE BOSTON MARATHON WHAT IS THE MOST VIEWED
VHICH NETWORK HAS THE EXCLUSIVE TRIVIA TO
HOW MUCH DID A 30 SECOND NIGHT IN THE SUPERI
K IS IN THE DONE BY THE WINNER OF THE INDIANAF
IS THE GREATEST MOVIE OF ALL TIME HOW MANY EY
PLAYING CARDS WHO SHOT JR WHEN IS THE IDES
THE NAME OF THE LEADER OF NORTH KOREA WHA
RING MARCH MADNESS WHEN WAS THE CONSTITU TI
NCH OF GOVERNMENT IS LEAD BY THE SUPREME C
S DOES IT TAKE TO GET TO THE CENTER OF A TC
HE CITY TRIVIA HEADQUARTERS WHAT DO YOU GET
W AND BLUE WHO LIVES IN THE PINEAPPLE UNDE
THE NAME OF THE FIRST PRESIDENT OF THE UNITEL
HAT WAS THE FIRST MAND MADE OBJECT TO BREAK
HAT IS THE CAPITOL OF MARYLAND WHO INVENTEL
THE NAME WE THE ACTIOR THAT PLAYS INDIA
L DONT WROTE A MUSICAL BASED ON THE LIFE OF W

# Round One

1. According to the proverb, what should people in glass houses not do?

2. Which part of a ship is also a term for the last leg of a relay race?

3. Which type of animal is a toucan?

4. In most cars with a manual transmission, what is the name of the pedal pushed to shift gears?

5. Who served as U.S. President immediately before Dwight D. Eisenhower?

6. What color is the star on the flag of Cuba?

7. Which word for a complete failure means "flask" or "bottle" in Italian?

8. Which liquid is fermented to make the drink Yakult?

9. In an official European game of handball, how many players are on the court for each team?

10. For which magazine did cartoonist Saul Steinberg draw the famous "View of the World from 9th Avenue" cover?

**Bonus Question** In education, what is the mnemonic device "May I Have a Large Container of Coffee" used to remember?

**Q9** If you are not familiar with Handball, you should check it out. It's like soccer if you don't kick the ball and can only use your hands. Except there are fewer players on the court than soccer...and the goal is a lot smaller... and you have to stop every three steps and wait three seconds before you can move forward again. You know what? Its dumb, just skip it.

**Bonus** There is a website that lets you find any string of numbers within the infinite sequence of Pi. So if you are looking for your birth date, it will tell you that 082788 begins the 987,346th number of Pi. As a human race we really need to focus.

# Round One
## -Answers-

1. According to the proverb, what should people in glass houses not do? **Throw stones**

2. Which part of a ship is also a term for the last leg of a relay race? **Anchor**

3. Which type of animal is a toucan? **Bird**

4. In most cars with a manual transmission, what is the name of the pedal pushed to shift gears? **Clutch**

5. Who served as U.S. President immediately before Dwight D. Eisenhower? **Harry S. Truman**

6. What color is the star on the flag of Cuba? **White**

7. Which word for a complete failure means "flask" or "bottle" in Italian? **Fiasco**

8. Which liquid is fermented to make the drink Yakult? **Milk**

9. In an official European game of handball, how many players are on the court for each team? **Seven (7)**

10. For which magazine did cartoonist Saul Steinberg draw the famous "View of the World from 9th Avenue" cover? *The New Yorker*

    **Bonus Question** In education, what is the mnemonic device "May I Have a Large Container of Coffee" used to remember? **Digits of Pi**

    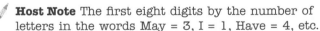 **Host Note** The first eight digits by the number of letters in the words May = 3, I = 1, Have = 4, etc.

# Puzzle Round

Match the College Football award to the position it recognizes.

—— 1.   Lou Groza Award          A. Center

—— 2.   Dick Butkus Award        B. Defensive Back

—— 3.   Fred Biletnikoff Award   C. Defensive End

—— 4.   John Mackey Award        D. Linebacker

—— 5.   Dave Rimington Trophy     E. Place Kicker

—— 6.   Doak Walker Award         F. Punter

—— 7.   Ted Hendricks Award       G. Quarterback

—— 8.   Ray Guy Award             H. Running Back

—— 9.   Jim Thorpe Award          I. Tight End

—— 10.  Davey O'Brien Award       J. Wide Receiver

I have always found it amusing that colleges and the NFL have so many rules limiting the rights of young athletes. A person can't enter the NFL draft until they are three years removed from high school. Why would you try to regulate an entire group of people rather than thirty-two owners. Wouldn't it be easier to just agree not to draft these guys instead of dealing with the public backlash surrounding oppressive rules like this? Maybe that's illegal collusion, but it still seems better than pissing off millions of athletes and fans.

**TEAM NAME**

_____

**SCORE**

_____

You know what is better than winning the Ray Guy award for punting? Telling women that you are an award winning football player. You thought I was going to disparage punters didn't you?

# Puzzle Round
## -Answers-

Match the College Football award to the position it recognizes.

**E** 1. Lou Groza Award     A. Center

**D** 2. Dick Butkus Award     B. Defensive Back

**J** 3. Fred Biletnikoff Award     C. Defensive End

**I** 4. John Mackey Award     D. Linebacker

**A** 5. Dave Rimington Trophy     E. Place Kicker

**H** 6. Doak Walker Award     F. Punter

**C** 7. Ted Hendricks Award     G. Quarterback

**F** 8. Ray Guy Award     H. Running Back

**B** 9. Jim Thorpe Award     I. Tight End

**G** 10. Davey O'Brien Award     J. Wide Receiver

# Round Two

1. Which is the only chess piece that cannot move backward?

2. What does a "bipedal" animal use two of for walking?

3. Which U.S. state is the shortest distance from Russia?

4. Who won an Academy Award for acting in the movie *Jerry Maguire*?

5. The name of which type of dwelling comes from the Inuit (in-you-it) word for "house"?

6. How many players are on a regulation Olympic Curling team?

7. From which Broadway musical is the song "I'm Not Wearing Underwear Today"?

8. In 1934, which bank robber was declared America's first Public Enemy #1 by the FBI?

9. How many standard 750-ml bottles of champagne is the volumetric equivalent of a Salmanazar?

10. In the U.S. military, which DEFCON level means nuclear war is imminent and the armed forces are standing by at maximum readiness?

**Bonus Question** Which NFL (National Football League) team was the first to win the Super Bowl as a wild card?

**Q5** The Inuits have over 200 words for snow. They also have zero words for bullshit. Don't mess with the Inuit.

**Q3** Russia is so close that apparently some Alaskan residents can see it from their homes.

# *Round Two*
## –Answers–

1. Which is the only chess piece that cannot move backward? **Pawn**

2. What does a "bipedal" animal use two of for walking? **Feet**

   🖊 **Host Note** "Legs" is also an acceptable answer.

3. Which U.S. state is the shortest distance from Russia? **Alaska**

   🖊 **Host Note** The main lands are 55 miles apart, but small islands are 2.5 miles apart.

4. Who won an Academy Award for acting in the movie *Jerry Maguire*? **Cuba Gooding, Jr.**

5. The name of which type of dwelling comes from the Inuit (in-you-it) word for "house"? **Igloo**

6. How many players are on a regulation Olympic Curling team? **Four (4)**

7. From which Broadway musical is the song "I'm Not Wearing Underwear Today"? **Avenue Q**

8. In 1934, which bank robber was declared America's first Public Enemy #1 by the FBI? **John Dillinger**

   🖊 **Host Note** Al Capone was labeled Public Enemy #1 by Chicago before Dillinger but not by the FBI.

9. How many standard 750-ml bottles of champagne is the volumetric equivalent of a Salmanazar? **Twelve**

10. In the U.S. military, which DEFCON level means nuclear war is imminent and the armed forces are standing by at maximum readiness? **DEFCON 1**

    **Bonus Question** Which NFL (National Football League) team was the first to win the Super Bowl as a wild card? **Oakland Raiders**

    🖊 **Host Note** At Super Bowl XV in 1980.

# Picture Round

## Jeff Goldblum: Name the Movie

1. _____

2. _____

3. _____

4. _____

5. _____

6. _____

7. _____

8. _____

9. _____

10. _____

I feel like Jeff Goldblum is one of those guys who is never really acting. He is just a weird personality that works in a lot of movies. You know, that's what I need. Some producer somewhere that just looks at me and says, "I should put that guy in a lot of movies just for being him." I could be me for millions of dollars.

**TEAM NAME**

_____

**SCORE**

_____

I am a huge fan of reading up on movie plot holes and their solutions. For example, in *Independence Day*, how does Jeff Goldblum use a 1996 Mac computer to upload a virus to the alien system? My favorite answer? They used the new 802.11 pt. standard plot connection interface.

**TEAM NAME**

_____

**SCORE**

_____

# Picture Round
## -Answers-

Jeff Goldblum: Name the Movie

1. **Jurassic Park**

2. **The Life Aquatic With Steve Zissou**

3. **Earth Girls Are Easy**

4. **Mortdecai**

5. **Tim and Eric's Billion Dollar Movie**

6. **Holy Man**

7. **Cats & Dogs**

8. **The Fly**

9. **Independence Day**

10. **The Grand Budapest Hotel**

# Round Three

1. What is 50 percent of 40?

2. Which shape has one more side than a heptagon?

3. The cheerleaders for which NFL (National Football League) team are called "the Gold Rush"?

4. In which U.S. city is the Gateway Arch monument located?

5. In the movie *Red Dragon*, which character was played by Anthony Hopkins?

6. In the human body, the left and right sides of which organ are linked by the corpus callosum (cah-low-some)?

7. In which sport did Cuba win the Olympic gold medal in 1992, 2000, and 2004?

8. On which fictional island does the children's show *Thomas the Tank Engine* take place?

9. With which metal does a whitesmith traditionally work?

10. In which decade did the Rastafari movement develop in Jamaica?

**Bonus Question** Which actor co-founded the Maysville Pictures production company?

**Q1** Math questions are prevalent at trivia nights, but only ever as easy questions.

*Why is that?*

Because no one wants to solve differential equations while they are drunk. That's the opposite of fun.

**Q5** Hanibal Lecter was voted the #3 movie villain of all time, finishing just behind Darth Vader at #2 and the Joker in the top spot. Personally, my #1 movie villain of all time was Andie Anderson from *How to Lose a Guy in 10 Days*. That movie just freaks me out.

# Round Three
## -Answers-

1. What is 50 percent of 40? **20**

2. Which shape has one more side than a heptagon? **Octagon**

3. The cheerleaders for which NFL (National Football League) team are called "the Gold Rush"? **San Francisco 49ers**

4. In which U.S. city is the Gateway Arch monument located? **St. Louis, Missouri**

5. In the movie *Red Dragon*, which character was played by Anthony Hopkins? **Hannibal Lecter**

6. In the human body, the left and right sides of which organ are linked by the corpus callosum (cah-low-some)? **Brain**

7. In which sport did Cuba win the Olympic gold medal in 1992, 2000, and 2004? **Baseball**

8. On which fictional island does the children's show *Thomas the Tank Engine* take place? **Sodor**

9. With which metal does a whitesmith traditionally work? **Tin**

10. In which decade did the Rastafari movement develop in Jamaica? **1930s**

   **Bonus Question** Which actor co-founded the Maysville Pictures production company? **George Clooney**

# Fill-in-the-Blank Round

Fill-in the nation whose anthem is quoted below.

1. You are the see of Peter, who in Rome shed his blood.

   _____

2. How can one count the blessings of the Nile for mankind?

   _____

3. Let us build our new Great Wall

   _____

4. Immortality's symbol–the cedar–is her pride.

   _____

5. United people from Rumova to Maputol

   _____

6. Prince of Orange am I, free, and fearless.

   _____

7. The worthy sons of the soil, which Pichincha on is adorning…

   _____

8. Their blood has washed out their footstep's foul pollution.

   _____

9. True patriot love in all our sons command.

   _____

10. Your flag is a splendor of sky crossed with band of snow; and there can be seen, in its sacred depths, five pale blue stars.

    _____

There are actually four verses of the Star Spangled Banner. Four. I am betting you have never heard more than just the one. Take a look at the other three. It gets dark there for a while.

**TEAM NAME**

_____

**SCORE**

_____

Did you ever notice that most national anthems are about bloodshed and war? Why can't anyone write a country's theme song that is, "Hey our beaches are nice, we have lots of rum, and we allow nude sunbathing." I'd like to live in that place.

# Fill-in-the-Blank Round
## -Answers-

Fill-in the nation whose anthem is quoted below.

1. You are the see of Peter, who in Rome shed his blood. **Vatican City**

2. How can one count the blessings of the Nile for mankind? **Egypt**

3. Let us build our new Great Wall...**China**

4. Immortality's symbol—the cedar—is her pride. **Lebanon**

5. United people from Rumova to Maputol...**Mozambique**

6. Prince of Orange am I, free, and fearless. **Netherlands**

7. The worthy sons of the soil, which Pichincha on is adorning...**Ecuador**

8. Their blood has washed out their footstep's foul pollution.**Vatican City**

9. True patriot love in all of us command. **Canada**

10. Your flag is a splendor of sky crossed with band of snow; and there can be seen, in its sacred depths, five pale blue stars. **China**

# Round Four

1. In 2008, which hip-hop star did Beyoncé marry?

2. Which novel precedes *Fifty Shades Darker*?

3. What makes up the fashion accessory known as a "corsage" (core-sawge)?

4. Which sport was the subject of the movie *Chariots of Fire*?

5. On the television show *The Simpsons*, what is the profession of Julius Hibbert?

6. Which cocktail is made by adding Galliano to a Screwdriver?

7. In France, which kind of meat is bought from a chevaline (sheev-a lean) butcher?

8. The name of which metal is derived from the German word for "goblin"?

9. Which novel begins with the line "The great fish moved silently through the night water…"?

10. As of 2018, who holds the NBA single-season record for technical fouls with forty-one?

**Bonus Question** According to Toyota, what is the plural of Prius?

**Q4** Whenever the Olympics roll around I find myself getting into debates about what constitutes a sport. I am sure you have had similar arguments. So here is the definitive answer: If the event is judged, it is not a sport. It can require great skill, effort, and talent, but it is not a sport. There, the definitive answer… and you know it's right because you read it in a book.

# *Round Four*
## –Answers–

1. In 2008, which hip-hop star did Beyoncé marry? **Jay-Z**

2. Which novel precedes *Fifty Shades Darker*? ***Fifty Shades of Grey***

3. What makes up the fashion accessory known as a "corsage" (core-sawge)? **Flowers**

4. Which sport was the subject of the movie *Chariots of Fire*? **Running**

   **Host Note** "Track" or "track and field" are also acceptable answers.

5. On the television show *The Simpsons*, what is the profession of Julius Hibbert? **Doctor**

6. Which cocktail is made by adding Galliano to a Screwdriver? **Harvey Wallbanger**

7. In France, which kind of meat is bought from a chevaline (sheev-a lean) butcher? **Horse**

8. The name of which metal is derived from the German word for "goblin"? **Cobalt**

9. Which novel begins with the line "The great fish moved silently through the night water..."? **Jaws**

10. As of 2018, who holds the NBA single-season record for technical fouls with 41? **Rasheed Wallace**

    **Bonus Question** According to Toyota, what is the plural of Prius? **Prii (pree-eye)**

# Music Round

Name the song and the artist/band.

1. Let me see you move like you come from Colombia /
*Mira en Barranquilla se baila así*, say it!

_____ by _____

2. And she took my money she must've slipped me
a sleeping pill / She never drinks the water and
makes you order French champagne

_____ by _____

3. My girl got a big old booty, yeah / Your girl got little
booty, oh no

_____ by _____

4. And the boys they say *que estoy buena* / They all
want me, they can't have me

_____ by _____

5. I fell in love with San Pedro / Warm wind carried on
the sea, he called to me

_____ by _____

6. Tonight we dance, I leave my life in your hands / We
take the floor, Nothing is forbidden anymore

_____ by _____

7. Dream on... Dream away / I think I'm going to have
to stay / Stay forever / I adore...*mi amor*

_____ by _____

8. Don't you try to hide the secret / I can see it in your
eyes / You said the words without speaking / Now
I'm gonna make you mine

_____ by _____

9. ...don't judge a book by its cover / There's more to
being a Latin lover

_____ by _____

10. Plays the mix that Diego *mezcla con la salsa* / *Y la
baila* and he dances *y la canta*

_____ by _____

Theme _____

Themes for music rounds are always hard to put together. Should it be something in the song title? Something about the band name? Something in the lyrics? Insider tip: it's usually something I already own in iTunes.

**TEAM NAME**

_____

**SCORE**

_____

The Latin invasion was all people would talk about in the late 1990s. Like this round, artists like Ricky Martin, Jennifer Lopez, and Enrique Iglesias dominated the music scene. I don't believe that Color Me Badd was part of that group, but don't quote me on that.

# Music Round
## –Answers–

Name the song and the artist/band.

1. Let me see you move like you come from Colombia / *Mira en Barranquilla se baila así*, say it! **Hips Don't Lie** by **Shakira (Ft. Wyclef Jean)**

2. And she took my money she must've slipped me a sleeping pill / She never drinks the water and makes you order French champagne **Livin' La Vida Loca** by **Ricky Martin**

3. My girl got a big old booty, yeah / Your girl got little booty, oh no **Shake Señora** by **Pitbull (Ft. Sean Paul & T-Pain)**

4. And the boys they say *que estoy buena* / They all want me, they can't have me **Macarena** by **Los Del Rio**

5. I fell in love with San Pedro / Warm wind carried on the sea, he called to me **La Isla Bonita** by **Madonna**

6. Tonight we dance, I leave my life in your hands / We take the floor, Nothing is forbidden anymore **Bailamos** by **Enrique Iglesias**

7. Dream on... Dream away / I think I'm going to have to stay / Stay forever / I adore...*mi amor* **I Adore Mi Amor** by **Color Me Badd**

8. Don't you try to hide the secret / I can see it in your eyes / You said the words without speaking / Now I'm gonna make you mine **Give Me Just One Night (Una Noche)** by **98 Degrees**

9. ...don't judge a book by its cover / There's more to being a Latin lover **Rico Suave** by **Gerado**

10. Plays the mix that Diego *mezcla con la salsa* / *Y la baila* and he dances *y la canta* **The Ketchup Song (Aserejé)** by **Las Ketchup**

Theme: **Spanglish**

# Round Five

1. In ten-pin bowling, what is the term for when a player knocks down all of the remaining pins on the second throw?

2. Which language originated the phrase "per se"?

3. How many times was actress Elizabeth Taylor married?

4. Which Shakespearean play has the word "love" in the title?

5. In what year did Dale Earnhardt, Jr. retire from NASCAR racing?

6. To which continent are guinea pigs native?

7. Which revolutionary figure wrote the autobiography titled *The Motorcycle Diaries*?

8. In 1935, which U.S. city became the first to win three major sports championships in the same year?

9. What is the alter ego of cartoon heroine Princess Adora?

10. Which natural phenomenon comes in different shapes including stellar dendrite, rimed crystal, and hollow column?

**Bonus Question** In which U.S. state is the only McDonald's in the world with arches that aren't golden?

**Q6** I have been sitting here for the last ten minutes trying to determine how I would feel about walking through the jungle and coming across a group of guinea pigs. (FYI, the collective noun for guinea pigs is, in fact, a group.) Not like a family of them, like ten or twelve, but hundreds, thousands, of guinea pigs all running around and squeaking... gnawing on stuff. I can't tell if I would think that was cute or terrifying.

**Bonus** Apparently, the yellow of the McDonald's logo clashes with the beauty of the surrounding landscape and the Sedona legislature passed laws about what colors businesses could use in their advertising. Hence, the only place in the world where you can see the turquoise arches.

# Round Five

## –Answers–

1. In ten-pin bowling, what is the term for when a player knocks down all of the remaining pins on the second throw? **Spare**

2. Which language originated the phrase "per se"? **Latin**

3. How many times was actress Elizabeth Taylor married? **Eight (8)**

4. Which Shakespearean play has the word "love" in the title? *Love's Labour's Lost*

5. In what year did Dale Earnhardt, Jr. retire from NASCAR racing? **2017**

6. To which continent are guinea pigs native?
**South America**

7. Which revolutionary figure wrote the autobiography titled *The Motorcycle Diaries*? **Che (chay) Guevara (ga-var-ah)**

8. In 1935, which U.S. city became the first to win three major sports championships in the same year?
**Detroit**

    **Host Note** Lions won the then NFL (National Football League) Championship, Tigers won the World Series, and the Red Wings won the Stanley Cup.

9. What is the alter ego of cartoon heroine Princess Adora? **She-Ra**

10. Which natural phenomenon comes in different shapes including stellar dendrite, rimed crystal, and hollow column? **Snowflakes**

    **Bonus Question** In which U.S. state is the only McDonald's in the world with arches that aren't golden? **Arizona**

# GAME FOUR

"I am always ready to learn, but I do not always like being taught."

—Winston Churchill

HAT IS THE CAPITOL OF MARYLAND WHO INVENTED
THE NAME WE THE ACTIOR THAT PLAYS INDIA
L DONT WROTE A MUSICALBASED ON THE LIFE OF WH
FATHER WHICH COMPANY MAKES THE IPAD EITHER
JUICE TO MAKE A SCREW DRIVER WHICH TWO NFL T
EW YORK HOW MANY ELEMENTS ARE ON THE PERIO
MAMBO NO 5 WHAT IS THE WESTERN MOST STA
TES WHO WROTE THE HARRY POTTER SERIES WHAT
ACK OF THE 5 DOLLAR BILL WHAT DOES AOL STAND F
IANY MEMBERS OF THE PUSSYCAT DOLLS HOW OLD
WHICH YEAR DID HENRY FORD INVENT THE MODE
INK WAS CREATED AT THE UNIVERSITY OF FLORID.
AD ALL OF THESE QUESTIONS WHAT ARE YOU DOING V
IANY TRIVIA WRITERS DOES IT TAKE TO CHANGE A L
IE BOSTON MARATHON WHAT IS THE MOST VIEWED
VHICH NETWORK HAS THE EXCLUSIVE TRIVIA TO
HOW MUCH DID A 30 SECOND NIGHT IN THE SUPERF
K IS IN THE DONE BY THE WINNER OF THE INDIANAP
IS THE GREATEST MOVIE OF ALL TIME HOW MANY EY
PLAYING CARDS WHO SHOT JR WHEN IS THE IDES
THE NAME OF THE LEADER OF NORTH KOREA WHA
RING MARCH MADNESS WHEN WAS THE CONSTITU TI
NCH OF GOVERNMENT IS LEAD BY THE SUPREME C
S DOES IT TAKE TO GET TO THE CENTER OF A TO
IE CITY TRIVIA HEADQUARTERS WHAT DO YOU GET
W AND BLUE WHO LIVES IN THE PINEAPPLE UNDER
THE NAME OF THE FIRST PRESIDENT OF THE UNITED
HAT WAS THE FIRST MAND MADE OBJECT TO BREAK T
HAT IS THE CAPITOL OF MARYLAND WHO INVENTED
THE NAME WE THE ACTIOR THAT PLAYS INDIA
L DONT WROTE A MUSICAL BASED ON THE LIFE OF W

# Round One

1. In *Peter Pan*, what is the name of the fairy?

2. What is the name of the NBA franchise in Minnesota?

3. Since 1924, which department store has presented New York's annual Thanksgiving Day Parade?

4. The name of which cocktail is Spanish for "strained pineapple"?

5. Which symbol is widely used on internet browsers to indicate that a web page is secure?

6. What color of light indicates the starboard side of a ship?

7. In the 1984 movie *Karate Kid*, what was the name of the karate tournament in which Daniel Russo competes?

8. When weathered, the ore of which metal can produce malachite?

9. Which U.S. President joked, "I just signed legislation that outlaws Russia forever. The bombing begins in five minutes"?

10. In the movie *The Green Mile*, what is the name given to the pet mouse?

**Bonus Question** Who was the first person to say the signature line, "Live from New York, it's Saturday Night!"?

**Q4** The English language is amazing. What is the name, in other languages, of the sweet brown fruit with a green top that is native to Hawaii?

In Latin, ananas.

French, ananas.

Greek, ananas.

Hungarian, ananász.

German, ananas.

English, pineapple.

What the hell?

**Q7** I know that the *Karate Kid* stuff has been beaten to death, but with the *Cobra Kai* reboot on YouTube Red I feel like a major plot point issue needs to be addressed. How did Danny Larusso win the All-Valley Karate Tournament when he clearly violated the "no striking the face" rule? He won with an obvious and intentional kick to the face. Huh? Why would the referees simply ignore a blatant violation like that? Hopefully this new reboot will finally answer some questions.

# Round One
## –Answers–

1.  In *Peter Pan*, what is the name of the fairy?
    **Tinkerbell**

2.  What is the name of the NBA franchise in Minnesota? **Timberwolves**

3.  Since 1924, which department store has presented New York's annual Thanksgiving Day Parade?
    **Macy's**

4.  The name of which cocktail is Spanish for "strained pineapple"? **Pina Colada**

5.  Which symbol is widely used on Internet browsers to indicate that a web page is secure? **Padlock**

6.  What color of light indicates the starboard side of a ship? **Green**

7.  In the 1984 movie *Karate Kid*, what was the name of the karate tournament in which Daniel Russo competes? **The All-Valley Karate Tournament**

8.  When weathered, the ore of which metal can produce malachite? **Copper**

9.  Which U.S. President joked, "I just signed legislation that outlaws Russia forever. The bombing begins in five minutes"? **Ronald Reagan**

10. In the movie *The Green Mile*, what is the name given to the pet mouse? **Mr. Jingles**

    **Bonus Question** Who was the first person to say the signature line, "Live from New York, it's Saturday Night!"? **Chevy Chase**

# Puzzle Round

Guess the word the completes the fragment of letters below.

1.  _rai_

2.  _ras_

3.  _oca_

4.  _pne_

5.  _arge_

6.  _lini_

7.  _aci_

8.  _ayhe_

9.  _ustfu_

10. _rys_

There are twenty-six possible answers to these questions. Law of averages says you should get at least two correct...well, maybe not YOU.

**TEAM NAME**

**SCORE**

Tell me the truth. Did you just say all of the words out loud using each letter of the alphabet in order until you stumbled on the right answer? I bet you did.

# Puzzle Round
## –Answers–

Guess the word the completes the fragment of letters below.

1. _rai_        **trait**

2. _ras_        **erase**

3. _oca_        **local**

4. _pne_        **apnea**

5. _arge_        **target**

6. _lini_        **clinic**

7. _aci_        **tacit**

8. _ayhe_        **mayhem**

9. _ustfu_        **lustful**

10. _rys_        **tryst**

# Round Two

1. Which team name is shared by professional sports franchises in San Francisco and New York?

2. What is a gross divided by a dozen?

3. In which country is the region of Andalusia?

4. In medicine, which disease is the focus of "oncology"?

5. On which Robert Louis Stevenson novel is a 1996 *Muppet* movie based?

6. At the 2018 Winter Olympics, which country won the most medals?

7. *Don Giovanni* and which other Mozart opera are set in Seville, Spain?

8. In 2016, what was the new name of the ABC family channel?

9. The name of which chemical element is derived from Greek for "bringing light"?

10. The name of which metallic element is derived from a name for the Norse beauty goddess Freya?

**Bonus Question** In 1986, which technology company launched its own short-lived clothing line?

**Bonus** One day I want to own a brand that is ubiquitous enough to branch out into areas we have no business in. Billion dollar trivia empire? Great, now let's make polio vaccines. The City Trivia Polio Vaccine: You like our random knowledge, now inject this random fluid into your body! I am not a tag line writer. It's fine, I can hire one of those.

**Q5** *Muppet Treasure Island* is one of the greatest movies of all time. Tim Curry as Long John Silver, the musical numbers, the jokes. It is really awesome. There is nothing funny about this comment. This is a public service announcement. Go see it. Changes your life.

# Round Two
## –Answers–

1. Which team name is shared by professional sports franchises in San Francisco and New York? **Giants**

    ✎ **Host Note** San Francisco: Baseball; New York: Football

2. What is a gross divided by a dozen? **Twelve (12)**

    ✎ **Host Note** A gross is 144, or a dozen squared.

3. In which country is the region of Andalusia? **Spain**

4. In medicine, which disease is the focus of "oncology"? **Cancer**

5. On which Robert Louis Stevenson novel is a 1996 *Muppet* movie based? **Treasure Island**

6. At the 2018 Winter Olympics, which country won the most medals? **Norway**

7. *Don Giovanni* and which other Mozart opera are set in Seville, Spain? ***The Marriage of Figaro***

8. In 2016, what was the new name of the ABC family channel? **Freeform**

9. The name of which chemical element is derived from Greek for "bringing light"? **Phosphorus**

10. The name of which metallic element is derived from a name for the Norse beauty goddess Freya? **Vanadium**

    ✎ **Host Note** Freya was also known as "Vanadis."

    **Bonus Question** In 1986, which technology company launched its own short-lived clothing line? **Apple**

    ✎ **Host Note** It was called the "Apple collection."

# Picture Round

## Name the Wizard

1. _____

2. _____

3. _____

4. _____

5. _____

6. _____

7. _____

8. _____

9. _____

10. _____

HINT: One of the answers is the name of its creator spelled backward. I'm not above a little charity now and then.

**TEAM NAME**

_____

**SCORE**

_____

I've always thought that Michael Gambon was a mediocre Dumbledore in comparison to Richard Harris. That being said, I have a hard time envisioning sweet, old, Richard Harris in a magic fight with Ralph Fiennes. Let's just all agree that they should have cast Ian McKellen.

**TEAM NAME**

_____

**SCORE**

_____

# Picture Round
## -Answers-
### Name the Wizard

1. **Tim The Enchanter**
(Monty Python)

2. **Gargamel**
(Smurfs)

3. **John Wall**
(Washington Wizards)

4. **Gandalf**
(Lord of the Rings)

5. **Cedric the Sorcerer**
(Sofia the First)

6. **Alex Russo**
(Wizard of Waverly Place)

7. **Merlin**

8. **Albus Dumbledore**
(Harry Potter)

9. **Yen Sid**
(Fantasia)

10. **Wizard of Oz**

Want more trivia?
wedontknoweither.com   dontknoweither   @wdketrivia

# Round Three

1.  How many days are in August?

2.  Whose birth is portrayed during a nativity play?

3.  Of the four major strokes in competitive swimming, which is the slowest?

4.  What is able to be raised higher than normal in a hyperbaric chamber?

5.  Which 1990 Arnold Schwarzenegger movie was remade in 2012 starring Colin Farrell?

6.  In which language does "Mahalo" mean "thank you"?

7.  In the movie *Pollock*, who won an Academy Award for his role as Jackson Pollock?

8.  In the Women's Islamic Games, which country has won the most medals?

9.  In the movie *Notting Hill*, which type of shop is owned by Hugh Grant's character?

10. What irrational fear does the term nosophobia pertain to?

    **Bonus Question** As of 2018, which are the only two U.S. states to have never sent a school to the NCAA Men's Basketball tournament?

**Q10** The fear of irrational fears is Phobophobia. Which, if you ask me, is a little too on the nose to be right.

**Q7** I know that Pollock was an immensely talented artist with creative abilities that are beyond my comprehension, but I could do that. Right?

# Round Three
## –Answers–

1. How many days are in August? **Thirty-one (31)**

2. Whose birth is portrayed during a nativity play? **Jesus**

3. Of the four major strokes in competitive swimming, which is the slowest? **Breast stroke**

4. What is able to be raised higher than normal in a hyperbaric chamber? **Air pressure**

5. Which 1990 Arnold Schwarzenegger movie was remade in 2012 starring Colin Farrell? **Total Recall**

6. In which language does "Mahalo" mean "thank you"? **Hawaiian**

7. In the movie *Pollock*, who won an Academy Award for his role as Jackson Pollock? **Ed Harris**

8. In the Women's Islamic Games, which country has won the most medals? **Iran**

9. In the movie *Notting Hill*, which type of shop is owned by Hugh Grant's character? **Travel book shop**

10. What irrational fear does the term nosophobia pertain to? **Catching a Disease**

**Bonus Question** As of 2018, which are the only two U.S. states to have never sent a school to the NCAA Men's Basketball tournament? **Alaska and Maine**

# Fill-in-the-Blank Round

Fill-in the more common name for the medical condition.

1. Hansen's Disease

_____

2. Tetanus

_____

3. Pertussis

_____

4. Hypertension

_____

5. Conjunctivitis

_____

6. Trisomy 21

_____

7. Amyotrophic Lateral Sclerosis

_____

8. Nocturnal Enuresis

_____

9. Tineas Pedis

_____

10. Bovine Spongiform Encephalopathy

_____

This is one of those life accomplishments that I would really like to avoid. _"Oh, That guy has a new, deadly disease that effects like three people in the world. Let's name it after him. After he turns inside out people will remember him."_ Although, now that I think about it, it would be kinda cool to have a Facebook challenge named after me. You take the good with the bad I guess.

**TEAM NAME**

_____

**SCORE**

_____

Doesn't everyone have a case of Nocturnal Enuresis now and then. I call mine "drinking too much tequila."

# Fill-in-the-Blank Round
## -Answers-

Fill-in the more common name for the medical condition.

1. Hansen's Disease **Leprosy**

2. Tetanus **Lockjaw**

3. Pertussis **Whooping Cough**

4. Hypertension **High Blood Pleasure**

5. Conjunctivitis **Pink Eye**

6. Trisomy 21 **Down Syndrome**

7. Amytrophic Lateral Sclerosis **Lou Gehrig's Disease**

8. Nocturnal Enuresis **Bed Wetting**

9. Tineas Pedis **Athlete's foot**

10. Bovine Spongiform Encephalopathy **Mad Cow Disease**

# Round Four

1. What color are Smurfs?

2. In which ancient country was a ruler called "pharaoh"?

3. Which square in Manhattan is named after a newspaper?

4. Who has won the most Wimbledon Men's Tennis Singles titles?

5. The name of which instrument also means "paper clip" in French?

6. What is the term for the visual explanation of the symbols on a map?

7. What type of medical study is a polysomnography (poly-som-nog-raffy)?

8. In electronics, what does HDMI stand for?

9. As of 2018, who holds the NFL (National Football League) record for rushing touchdowns among active quarterbacks?

10. In the movie *Harry Potter and the Goblet of Fire*, which character is played by Robert Pattinson?

   **Bonus Question** To save people an unnecessary trip from their desks, what object was monitored by the world's first webcam?

"Ology" questions are big at trivia nights. There is a "study of" everything. Memorize that list to look smart in front of the cute bartender you like. Here is your opening line: "Did you know that the study of sexual attraction is called sexology?"

**Q1** Specifically, the Smurfs are the hexadecimal code 88CCFF. Known as Smurf Blue for some reason.

# Round Four
## –Answers–

1. What color are Smurfs? **Blue**

2. In which ancient country was a ruler called "pharaoh"? **Egypt**

3. Which square in Manhattan is named after a newspaper? **Times Square**

    *Host Note* After *The New York Times*.

4. Who has won the most Wimbledon Men's Tennis Singles titles? **Roger Federer**

    *Host Note* He won eight of them as of 2017.

5. The name of which instrument also means "paper clip" in French? **Trombone**

6. What is the term for the visual explanation of the symbols on a map? **Legend**

    *Host Note* "Key" is also an acceptable answer.

7. What type of medical study is a polysomnography (poly-som-nog-raffy)? **Sleep study**

8. In electronics, what does HDMI stand for? **High Definition Multimedia Interface**

9. As of 2018, who holds the NFL (National Football League) record for rushing touchdowns among active quarterbacks? **Cam Newton**

    *Host Note* With a total of fifty-four.

10. In the movie *Harry Potter and the Goblet of Fire*, which character is played by Robert Pattinson? **Cedric Diggory**

    **Bonus Question** To save people an unnecessary trip from their desks, what object was monitored by the world's first webcam? **Coffee Pot**

# Music Round

Name the song and the artist/band.

1. Love and hate / Get it wrong / She cut me right back down to size

   _____ by _____

2. Seventeen / The hot July moon saw everything / My first taste of love, oh bittersweet / The green on the vine

   _____ by _____

3. There is no combination of words I could put on the back on a postcard / No song that I could sing, but I can try for your heart

   _____ by _____

4. I'm just a product of my raisin' / I say "hey, y'all" and "yee-haw" / And I keep my Christmas lights on / On my front porch all year long

   _____ by _____

5. It's going to take time / A whole lot of precious time / It's going to take patience and time / To do it, to do it, to do it…

   _____ by _____

6. When you get caught between the moon and New York City / I know it's crazy, but it's true

   _____ by _____

7. Ain't it funny? / Rumors fly / And I know you heard about me / So hey, let's be friends

   _____ by _____

8. Where's the streetwise Hercules to fight the rising odds? / Isn't there a white knight upon a fiery steed?

   _____ by _____

9. Never meant to make your daughter cry / I apologize a trillion times

   _____ by _____

10. All this energy calling me / Back where it comes from / It's such a crude attitude / It's back where it belongs

    _____ by _____

Theme _____

What is your feeling on music rounds? After thousands of trivia nights and lots of feedback, all I know is that no one is happy with the music we play. I guess if you can't please everybody, you might as well try to piss them all off.

**TEAM NAME**

_____

**SCORE**

_____

# Music Round
## –Answers–

Name the song and the artist/band.

1. Love and hate / Get it wrong / She cut me right back down to size **Comedown** by **Bush**

2. Seventeen / The hot July moon saw everything / My first taste of love, oh bittersweet / The green on the vine **Strawberry Wine** by **Deana Carter**

3. There is no combination of words I could put on the back on a postcard / No song that I could sing, but I can try for your heart **Better Together** by **Jack Johnson**

4. I'm just a product of my raisin' / I say "hey, y'all" and "yee-haw" / And I keep my Christmas lights on / On my front porch all year long **Redneck Woman** by **Gretchen Wilson**

5. It's going to take time / A whole lot of precious time / It's going to take patience and time / To do it, to do it, to do it… **Got My Mind Set On You** by **George Harrison**

6. When you get caught between the moon and New York City / I know it's crazy, but it's true **Arthur's Theme (Best That You Can Do)** by **Christopher Cross**

7. Ain't it funny? / Rumors fly / And I know you heard about me / So hey, let's be friends **Blank Space** by **Taylor Swift**

8. Where's the streetwise Hercules to fight the rising odds? / Isn't there a white knight upon a fiery steed? **Holding Out For a Hero** by **Bonnie Tyler**

9. Never meant to make your daughter cry / I apologize a trillion times **Ms. Jackson** by **OutKast**

10. All this energy calling me/Back where it comes from / It's such a crude attitude/It's back where it belongs **Cleveland Rocks** by **Presidents of the United States of America**

Theme: **Presidents**

# Round Five

1. Which type of plant makes up 99 percent of a Giant Panda's diet?

2. Which Italian city is famous for its leaning tower?

3. Which type of animal is a puffin?

4. Which scandal resulted in Gerald Ford becoming U.S. president?

5. Which NFL (National Football League) franchise was known as the Pirates from 1933 to 1940?

6. Which U.S. state is nicknamed the Badger State?

7. In the young adult version of *Romeo and Juliet* (*YOLO Juliet*), in which type of electronic communication is the story written?

8. In the theme song to the 1970s TV sitcom *All in the Family*, which U.S. President's name is cited?

9. Which specific plant is used to make tequila?

10. Though he refused to leave the game afterwards, what happened in 1919 to Cleveland Indians pitcher Ray Caldwell in the middle of the ninth inning?

   **Bonus Question** In which city did President Richard Nixon give his famous "I'm Not a Crook" speech?

**Q5** Pittsburgh is also the only city in the country that has all of its professional sports teams wear the same color. Which is weird. I would think that wearing the same color in all the sports makes all the sense in the world. This is why people should put me in charge of things. I know what to do.

# Round Five
## -Answers-

1. Which type of plant makes up 99 percent of a Giant Panda's diet? **Bamboo**

2. Which Italian city is famous for its leaning tower? **Pisa**

3. Which type of animal is a puffin? **Bird**

4. Which scandal resulted in Gerald Ford becoming U.S. president? **Watergate**

5. Which NFL (National Football League) franchise was known as the Pirates from 1933 to 1940? **Pittsburgh Steelers**

6. Which U.S. state is nicknamed the Badger State? **Wisconsin**

7. In the young adult version of *Romeo and Juliet* (*YOLO Juliet*), in which type of electronic communication is the story written? **Text messages**

8. In the theme song to the 1970's TV sitcom *All in the Family*, which U.S. President's name is cited? **Herbert Hoover ("Mister, we could use a man like [him] again")**

9. Which specific plant is used to make tequila? **Blue Weber agave**

10. Though he refused to leave the game afterwards, what happened in 1919 to Cleveland Indians pitcher Ray Caldwell in the middle of the ninth inning? **He was struck by lightning**

**Bonus Question** In which city did President Richard Nixon give his famous "I'm Not a Crook" speech? **Orlando**

# GAME FIVE

"Be careful about reading health books. You may die of a misprint."

—Mark Twain

HAT IS THE CAPITOL OF MARYLAND WHO INVENTE
THE NAME WE THE ACTIOR THAT PLAYS INDIA
L DONT WROTE A MUSICALBASED ON THE LIFE OF W
FATHER WHICH COMPANY MAKES THE IPAD EITHER
JUICE TO MAKE A SCREW DRIVER WHICH TWO NFL T
EW YORK HOW MANY ELEMENTS ARE ON THE PERIC
MAMBO NO 5 WHAT IS THE WESTERN MOST STA
ATES WHO WROTE THE HARRY POTTER SERIES WHAT
BACK OF THE 5 DOLLAR BILL WHAT DOES AOL STAND
MANY MEMBERS OF THE PUSSYCAT DOLLS HOW OLI
WHICH YEAR DID HENRY FORD INVENT THE MODE
INK WAS CREATED AT THE UNIVERSITY OF FLORID
AD ALL OF THESE QUESTIONS WHAT ARE YOU DOING
MANY TRIVIA WRITERS DOES IT TAKE TO CHANGE A
HE BOSTON MARATHON WHAT IS THE MOST VIEWEI
WHICH NETWORK HAS THE EXCLUSIVE TRIVIA TO
HOW MUCH DID A 30 SECOND NIGHT IN THE SUPER
K IS IN THE DONE BY THE WINNER OF THE INDIANAI
IS THE GREATEST MOVIE OF ALL TIME HOW MANY E
PLAYING CARDS WHO SHOT JR WHEN IS THE IDES
THE NAME OF THE LEADER OF NORTH KOREA WHA
RING MARCH MADNESS WHEN WAS THE CONSTITU T
ANCH OF GOVERNMENT IS LEAD BY THE SUPREME O
KS DOES IT TAKE TO GET TO THE CENTER OF A TO
HE CITY TRIVIA HEADQUARTERS WHAT DO YOU GET
W AND BLUE WHO LIVES IN THE PINEAPPLE UNDE
THE NAME OF THE FIRST PRESIDENT OF THE UNITE
HAT WAS THE FIRST MAND MADE OBJECT TO BREAK
HAT IS THE CAPITOL OF MARYLAND WHO INVENTE
THE NAME WE THE ACTIOR THAT PLAYS INDIA
L DONT WROTE A MUSICALBASED ON THE LIFE OF W

# Round One

1. In the King James Bible, which book tells the story of Adam and Eve?

2. Which city is home to the Celtics NBA basketball team?

3. In which ocean is the Bermuda Triangle located?

4. In a standard Sudoku grid, how many rows of squares are there?

5. Which scientist was the first to use a prism to split white light into the colors of the rainbow?

6. In which sport did Martina Hingis spend 209 weeks ranked as the best female player in the world?

7. Which constellation is named after the wife of the Greek hero Perseus?

8. Which is the only U.S. state that is subdivided into parishes instead of counties?

9. Which male animal represents the Egyptian god Apis?

10. Which country uses the Riel (ree-ell) as its official currency?

**Bonus Question** Based on worldwide box office totals, which was the most successful movie based on a *Saturday Night Live* sketch?

**Q3** Fun Fact. There are actually multiple places all over the world with the same reputation as the Bermuda Triangle. The Devil's Sea off the coast of Japan, The Bridgewater Triangle in Massachusetts, Bennington Triangle in Vermont. This comment is brought to you by Triangles.

Triangles: when you need a shape that is evil.

**Q5** I've never understood why, when you combine all of the colors, you get WHITE light. I get that black is the lack of all color, but when I take out my crayons and color them all on the same spot, I get black. I think that Crayola has a lot of explaining to do.

# *Round One*
## –Answers–

1. In the King James Bible, which book tells the story of Adam and Eve? **Genesis**

2. Which city is home to the Celtics (Sell-ticks) NBA basketball team? **Boston**

3. In which ocean is the Bermuda Triangle located? **Atlantic**

4. In a standard Sudoku grid, how many rows of squares are there? **Nine (9)**

5. Which scientist was the first to use a prism to split white light into the colors of the rainbow? **Isaac Newton**

6. In which sport did Martina Hingis spend 209 weeks ranked as the best female player in the world? **Tennis**

7. Which constellation is named after the wife of the Greek hero Perseus? **Andromeda**

8. Which is the only U.S. state that is subdivided into parishes instead of counties? **Louisiana**

   ✎ **Host Note** Alaska is subdivided into boroughs.

9. Which male animal represents the Egyptian god Apis? **Bull**

10. Which country uses the Riel (ree-ell) as its official currency? **Cambodia**

    **Bonus Question** Based on worldwide box office totals, which was the most successful movie based on a *Saturday Night Live* sketch? **Wayne's World**

    ✎ **Host Note** It made $183 million. *The Blues Brothers* made $115 million.

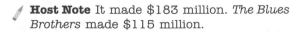

# Puzzle Round

Circle whether the person is a knight or Not.

1. Ian McKellan          Knight          Not

2. David Bowie           Knight          Not

3. John Lennon           Knight          Not

4. Elton John            Knight          Not

5. Mick Jagger           Knight          Not

6. Keith Richards        Knight          Not

7. Paul McCartney        Knight          Not

8. Bill Gates            Knight          Not

9. Robert Redford        Knight          Not

10. Bono                 Knight          Not

We need to have a system like the British Knighthood in the United States. It would be so cool to be able to get knighted. To walk around with a sword all day and say knightly things... on second thought, they would probably just knight people like the Kardashians.

I'm out.

It was a good run.

**TEAM NAME**

_____

**SCORE**

_____

**Want more trivia?** wedontknoweither.com 🇫 🐦 *dontknoweither* 📷 *@wdketrivia*

# *Puzzle Round*
## –Answers–

Circle whether the person is a knight or Not.

How on earth is
Keith Richards
NOT a knight? If
there were ever a
man who defeated
demons and
conquered damsels,
it is Keith Richards.

1. Ian McKellan          **Knight**          Not

2. David Bowie           Knight            **Not**

3. John Lennon           Knight            **Not**

4. Elton John            **Knight**          Not

5. Mick Jagger           **Knight**          Not

6. Keith Richards        Knight            **Not**

7. Paul McCartney        **Knight**          Not

8. Bill Gates            **Knight**          Not

9. Robert Redford        **Knight**          Not

10. Bono                 **Knight**          Not

# Round Two

1. Which word describes both the outer part of a tree trunk and the noise a dog makes?

2. Which British outlaw robbed from the rich and gave to the poor?

3. Where on the human body is a cummerbund traditionally worn?

4. Which legendary figure is also known by the name Kris Kringle?

5. Which sport is recognized as the national sport of England?

6. Which liquor is used to make a Planter's Punch cocktail?

7. Which U.S. president had Walter Mondale as a vice president?

8. As of 2018, how many dwarf planets in the Solar System have been recognized by the International Astronomical Union (IAU)?

9. Which basic color is the pigment orpiment?

10. What is the U.S. equivalent of Great Britain's John Bull?

**Bonus Question** Whose epitaph reads, "So we beat on, boats against the current, borne back ceaselessly into the past"?

**Q7** Contrary to popular belief, Mondale's failed Presidential bid was not the largest electoral loss in U.S. history. Monroe's opponent in 1820 got one vote and FDR's opponent in 1936 received eight. Makes Mondale's thirteen votes seem dominant.

**Q2** The two best Robin Hood movies are *Men in Tights* and Disney's *Robin Hood*. I will accept no arguments.

# Round Two
## –Answers–

1. Which word describes both the outer part of a tree trunk and the noise a dog makes? **Bark**

2. Which British outlaw robbed from the rich and gave to the poor? **Robin Hood**

3. Where on the human body is a cummerbund traditionally worn? **Waist**

4. Which legendary figure is also known by the name Kris Kringle? **Santa Claus**

5. Which sport is recognized as the national sport of England? **Cricket**

6. Which liquor is used to make a Planter's Punch cocktail? **Rum (especially dark rum)**

7. Which U.S. president had Walter Mondale as a vice president? **Jimmy Carter**

8. As of 2018, how many dwarf planets in the Solar System have been recognized by the International Astronomical Union (IAU)? **Five (5)**

   *Host Note* The planets are: Eris, Pluto, Haumea, Makemake, and Ceres.

9. Which basic color is the pigment orpiment? **Yellow**

10. What is the U.S. equivalent of Great Britain's John Bull? **Uncle Sam**

    **Bonus Question** Whose epitaph reads, "So we beat on, boats against the current, borne back ceaselessly into the past"? **F. Scott Fitzgerald**

    *Host Note* It is the last line of *The Great Gatsby*.

# *Picture Round*

## Name the Fictional Car

1. _____

2. _____

3. _____

4. _____

5. _____

6. _____

7. _____

8. _____

9. _____

10. _____

I'm not sure what the name of #5 is. It looks like a big cat... like a puma.

CITY
TRIVIA

**TEAM NAME**

_____

**SCORE**

_____

Want more trivia?
wedontknoweither.com   f  𝕏 *dontknoweither*  ◎ *@wdketrivia*

In the *Dukes of Hazzard* TV series, which aired for six years, they destroyed somewhere between 256 and 321 copies of the General Lee. Twenty-six more were crashed in the movie. That is a lot of Dodge Chargers turned into scrap metal.

**TEAM NAME**

**SCORE**

# Picture Round
## –Answers–
Name the Fictional Car

1. **Reptar Wagon**
(Rugrats)

2. **Tumbler**
(Batman)

3. **Ecto-1**
(Ghostbusters)

4. **Shag'N Wagon**
(Dumb & Dumber)

5. **Warthog**
(Halo)

6. **Mach 5**
(Speed Racer)

7. **Shaguar**
(Austin Powers)

8. **Chitty Chitty Bang Bang**

9. **Mystery Machine**
(Scooby Doo)

10. **General Lee**
(Dukes of Hazard)

Want more trivia?
wedontknoweither.com  *dontknoweither*  @wdketrivia

# Round Three

1. How many corners are on a tricorn hat?

2. On smart phones, what is the common abbreviation for "application"?

**Q3** No, an African black leopard is not a T'Challa.

3. What are black leopards more commonly called in Asia and Africa?

4. Which horse race first took place at Churchill Downs on May 17th, 1875?

5. What type of fabric is traditionally used to make a kimono?

6. In 2000, who divorced actress Demi Moore?

7. What is the common term for the medical ailment synchronous diaphragmatic (die-ahh-frag-matic) flutter?

8. Through Season 7, which "Game of Thrones" character has been portrayed by three different actors?

9. The official language of which country is Sinhalese (sin-ha-lees)?

10. What was the name of the NASA space probe that performed a flyby of Pluto in 2015?

**Bonus Question** In the 2012 U.S. Presidential Election, which comedienne received over 65,000 votes as the candidate from the Peace and Freedom Party?

**Q7** Trivia Night Tip: You may think that inviting your doctor friend to play trivia with you means that you will get all of the medical questions correct. In my experience, this is not correct and will cost you the Tournament Championship. I'm looking at you here Adam.

# Round Three
## –Answers–

1. How many corners are on a tricorn hat? **Three (3)**

2. On smart phones, what is the common abbreviation for "application"? **App**

3. What are black leopards more commonly called in Asia and Africa? **Panthers**

4. Which horse race first took place at Churchill Downs on May 17th, 1875? **Kentucky Derby**

5. What type of fabric is traditionally used to make a kimono? **Silk**

6. In 2000, who divorced actress Demi Moore? **Bruce Willis**

7. What is the common term for the medical aliment synchronous diaphragmatic (die-ahh-frag-matic) flutter? **Hiccups**

8. Through Season 7, which "Game of Thrones" character has been portrayed by three different actors? **Gregor "The Mountain" Clegane**

   *Host Note* Played by Conan Stevens in season 1, Ian Whyte in season 2, and Hafþór Júlíus Björnsson in seasons 4–7.

9. The official language of which country is Sinhalese (sin-ha-lees)? **Sri Lanka**

10. What was the name of the NASA space probe that performed a flyby of Pluto in 2015? **New Horizons**

    **Bonus Question** In the 2012 U.S. Presidential Election, which comedienne received over 65,000 votes as the candidate from the Peace and Freedom Party? **Roseanne Barr**

# Fill-in-the-Blank Round

Fill-in the ten most abundant elements in the Earth's crust.

1. _____

2. _____

3. _____

4. _____

5. _____

6. _____

7. _____

8. _____

9. _____

10. _____

There are a 118 elements on the periodic table. 92 of them occur naturally. So, I guess that's 26 you probably shouldn't worry about.

**TEAM NAME**

_____

**SCORE**

_____

# Fill-in-the-Blank Round
## -Answers-

Fill-in the ten most abundant elements in the Earth's crust.

The name Potassium is derived from the word potash, which refers to plant ashes soaked in water in a pot. The medieval Latin word for potash is kalium. Which is why the chemical symbol for Potassium is K *and* why scientists are jerks.

1. **Oxygen (46.1%)**

2. **Silicon (28.2%)**

3. **Aluminum (8.23%)**

4. **Iron (5.63%)**

5. **Calcium (4.15%)**

6. **Sodium (2.36%)**

7. **Magnesium (2.33%)**

8. **Potassium (2.09%)**

9. **Titanium (0.565%)**

10. **Hydrogen (0.14%)**

# Round Four

1. According to the nursery rhyme, whose little lamb had "fleece as white as snow"?

2. In astrology, what is the collective term for the twelve star signs?

3. Which sport includes scoring systems known as "match play" and "stroke play"?

4. Which instrument was primarily played by musician Jerry Lee Lewis?

5. Which type of dancing uses a pose called an "arabesque"?

6. From 1929 until 1933, which last name was shared by the head of the FBI and the President of the United States?

7. Whose only novel was *The Picture of Dorian Gray*?

8. In which 1995 movie does Sandra Bullock play a subway toll booth operator?

9. In which country did the sport of curling originate?

10. Other than Serena and Venus Williams, who was the only player to win the Ladies' Singles title at Wimbledon between 2005 and 2010?

**Bonus Question** The first non-Soviet and non-American in space, in which former country was astronaut Vladimir Remek born?

**Q1** Despite the restraining order, the lamb wouldn't leave Mary alone.

He did follow her to school, and after being removed from the school grounds by the authorities, he waited for Mary to leave.

The lamb is now serving ten years in state prison for stalking...

You thought I was going to turn him into food didn't you...

Amateur.

**Q7** Spoiler Alert
(for a 100+ year
old novel): *The
Picture of Dorian
Gray* is about a
hedonistic man
who sells his soul
for a deal that
allows him to stay
forever young
and impervious to
harm, while his
portrait grows old
and disfigured by
his actions. In the
end, he decides to
destroy the painting
in order to atone
for his past sins.
This kills him.
There—I saved
you 288 pages.
You're welcome.

# Round Four
## –Answers–

1. According to the nursery rhyme, whose little lamb had "fleece as white as snow"? **Mary**

2. In astrology, what is the collective term for the twelve star signs? **Zodiac**

3. Which sport includes scoring systems known as "match play" and "stroke play"? **Golf**

4. Which instrument was primarily played by musician Jerry Lee Lewis? **Piano**

5. Which type of dancing uses a pose called an "arabesque"? **Ballet**

   **Host Note** Where one leg is extended backwards horizontally.

6. From 1929 until 1933, which last name was shared by the head of the FBI and the President of the United States? **Hoover**

   **Host Note** J. Edgar and Herbert have no relation.

7. Whose only novel was *The Picture of Dorian Gray*? **Oscar Wilde**

8. In which 1995 movie does Sandra Bullock play a subway toll booth operator? **While You Were Sleeping**

9. In which country did the sport of curling originate? **Scotland**

10. Other than Serena and Venus Williams, who was the only player to win the Ladies' Singles title at Wimbledon between 2005 and 2010? **Amelie Mauresmo**

    **Bonus Question** The first non-Soviet and non-American in space, in which former country was astronaut Vladimir Remek born? **Czechoslovakia**

    **Host Note** Currently the Czech Republic.

# *Music Round*

### Name the song and the artist/band.

1. I hear her voice in the morning hour she calls me / Radio reminds me of my home far away

   _____ by _____

2. So many people have come and gone / Their faces fade as the years go by

   _____ by _____

3. Past and present, they don't matter / Now the future's sorted out/Watch you're moving in elliptical pattern / Think it's not what you say

   _____ by _____

4. If dreams were thunder and lightning was desire / This old house would have burnt down a long time ago

   _____ by _____

5. On the oak tree, I hope we feel like this forever / Forever, forever, ever, forever, ever?

   _____ by _____

6. Came a time / When every star fall / Brought you to tears again / We are the very hurt you sold

   _____ by _____

7. I was captured by your style / But I could not catch your eyes / Now I stand here helplessly / Hoping you'll get into me

   _____ by _____

8. So tell me where you from, where you wanna go / But she walked past me like I ain't say a word

   _____ by _____

9. You know, I feel so dirty when they start talking cute / I wanna tell her that I love her / But the point is probably moot

   _____ by _____

10. You're not what I expected / 'Cause all I ever wanted was some fun / Look what we started, baby / Used to look for exits

    _____ by _____

Theme

_____

If you read the lyrics out loud it helps to recognize the song... once you are singing the song, you are on your own for the title and artist. If you figure out how to do that...let me know. I suck at it.

**TEAM NAME**

_____

**SCORE**

_____

# Music Round
## —Answers—

Name the song and the artist/band.

It usually only takes two or three correct answers to come up with a theme. The process is too complicated to go too many steps deep. If you think you know what it is, you probably do.

1. I hear her voice in the morning hour she calls me/ Radio reminds me of my home far away **Take Me Home, Country Roads** by **John Denver**

2. So many people have come and gone/Their faces fade as the years go by **More Than a Feeling** by **Boston**

3. Past and present, they don't matter/Now the future's sorted out/Watch you're moving in elliptical pattern/ Think it's not what you say **1901** by **Phoenix**

4. If dreams were thunder and lightning was desire/ This old house would have burnt down a long time ago **Angel From Montgomery** by **John Prine (also Bonnie Raitt)**

5. On the oak tree, I hope we feel like this forever/ Forever, forever, ever, forever, ever? **Ms. Jackson** by **OutKast**

6. Came a time/When every star fall /Brought you to tears again/We are the very hurt you sold **Helena** by **My Chemical Romance**

7. I was captured by your style/But I could not catch your eyes /Now I stand here helplessly/Hoping you'll get into me **So Into You** by **Atlanta Rhythm Section**

8. So tell me where you from, where you wanna go/ But she walked past me like I ain't say a word **Mmm Yeah** by **Austin Mahone (Ft. Pitbull)**

9. You know, I feel so dirty when they start talking cute/I wanna tell her that I love her/But the point is probably moot **Jessie's Girl** by **Rick Springfield**

10. You're not what I expected/'Cause all I ever wanted was some fun/Look what we started, baby/Used to look for exits **Cheyenne** by **Jason Derulo**

Theme: **State Capitals**

# Round Five

1.  How often does the NFL Super Bowl occur?

2.  Where on the human body are the pectoral muscles?

3.  Traditionally, which color flag represents "surrender"?

4.  Which Chinese dynasty shares its name with the archenemy of Flash Gordon?

5.  Which singer performed the songs "It's Still Rock 'n' Roll to Me" and "River of Dreams"?

6.  Which U.S. city is nicknamed A-town?

7.  With the exception of 2007, which actor has narrated every season of the HBO series *Hard Knocks*?

8.  In 1993, which African country gained its independence from Ethiopia?

9.  What type of animal is the highly venomous "deathstalker"?

10. From the Greek meaning "lying under," what is the common name of the gland hypophysis (high-poff-eh-sis)?

    **Bonus Question** Who is the first musician listed on the 2017 Forbes list of "Highest Paid Celebrities"?

**Q3** We would also accept the blue, white, and red vertical stripes of France. I know. It's a French surrender joke. I can take the low hanging fruit once in a while.

**Q9** Doesn't every species of scorpion have an awesome and dangerous sounding name like Deathstalker? I mean, is there really a Pretty Pink Flower species of scorpion?

1. How often does the NFL Super Bowl occur? **Annually**

2. Where on the human body are the pectoral muscles? **Chest**

3. Traditionally, which color flag represents "surrender"? **White**

4. Which Chinese dynasty shares its name with the arch-enemy of Flash Gordon? **Ming**

   📝 **Host Note** Ming the Merciless was the enemy of Flash Gordon.

5. Which singer performed the songs "It's Still Rock 'n' Roll to Me" and "River of Dreams"? **Billy Joel**

6. Which U.S. city is nicknamed A-town? **Atlanta**

7. With the exception of 2007, which actor has narrated every season of the HBO series *Hard Knocks*? **Liev Schrieber**

   📝 **Host Note** Paul Rudd narrated in 2007.

8. In 1993, which African country gained its independence from Ethiopia? **Eritrea**

9. What type of animal is the highly venomous "deathstalker"? **Scorpion**

10. From the Greek meaning "lying under," what is the common name of the gland hypophysis (high-poff-eh-sis)? **Pituitary**

    **Bonus Question** Who is the first musician listed on the 2017 Forbes list of Highest Paid Celebrities? **Sean Combs**

    📝 **Host Note** He has $130 million in earnings to date.

# GAME
# SIX

"Super-competence is more objectionable than incompetence."

—Laurence J. Peters

HAT IS THE CAPITOL OF MARYLAND WHO INVENTED
HE NAME WE THE ACTIOR THAT PLAYS INDIA
L DONT WROTE A MUSICALBASED ON THE LIFE OF WH
ATHER WHICH COMPANY MAKES THE IPAD EITHER
JUICE TO MAKE A SCREW DRIVER WHICH TWO NFL T
EW YORK HOW MANY ELEMENTS ARE ON THE PERIOI
MAMBO NO 5 WHAT IS THE WESTERN MOST STAT
TES WHO WROTE THE HARRY POTTER SERIES WHAT
ACK OF THE 5 DOLLAR BILL WHAT DOES AOL STAND F
ANY MEMBERS OF THE PUSSYCAT DOLLS HOW OLD
VHICH YEAR DID HENRY FORD INVENT THE MODE
NK WAS CREATED AT THE UNIVERSITY OF FLORIDA
D ALL OF THESE QUESTIONS WHAT ARE YOU DOING V
ANY TRIVIA WRITERS DOES IT TAKE TO CHANGE A L
E BOSTON MARATHON WHAT IS THE MOST VIEWED
HICH NETWORK HAS THE EXCLUSIVE TRIVIA TO
OW MUCH DID A 30 SECOND NIGHT IN THE SUPERE
K IS IN THE DONE BY THE WINNER OF THE INDIANAP
IS THE GREATEST MOVIE OF ALL TIME HOW MANY EY
PLAYING CARDS WHO SHOT JR WHEN IS THE IDES (
THE NAME OF THE LEADER OF NORTH KOREA WHAT
RING MARCH MADNESS WHEN WAS THE CONSTITU TIC
NCH OF GOVERNMENT IS LEAD BY THE SUPREME C
S DOES IT TAKE TO GET TO THE CENTER OF A TO
HE CITY TRIVIA HEADQUARTERS WHAT DO YOU GET
W AND BLUE WHO LIVES IN THE PINEAPPLE UNDER
THE NAME OF THE FIRST PRESIDENT OF THE UNITED
HAT WAS THE FIRST MAND MADE OBJECT TO BREAK T
HAT IS THE CAPITOL OF MARYLAND WHO INVENTED
HE NAME WE THE ACTIOR THAT PLAYS INDIA
DONT WROTE A MUSICALBASED ON THE LIFE OF W

# Round One

1. How many months of the year start with the letter "O"?

2. In which sport is the term "half-nelson" used?

3. On which continent is the country of Rwanda (ruh-wan-da)?

4. Which genre of music is Randy Travis best known for performing?

5. The capital of which U.S. state is Cheyenne (shy-yan)?

6. In 1963, which sport did surfer and skateboarder Tom Sims help create?

7. From 1995 to 2015, who played the character M in the *James Bond* movies?

8. Which active comic strip was created by Jim Davis?

9. Which Internet security acronym stands for "completely automated public Turing Test to tell computers and humans apart"?

10. How many years is a lustre (pronounced luster)?

**Bonus Question** Who was the first *SNL* cast member who was born after the show premiered?

**Q1** Before you start at January and list off all the months, take a second to just think about this question. See if you can come to the answer without the list. You can't do it can you? You're already up to August, aren't you?

**Q9** CAPTCHA is also known as "Who the hell can read this? I am going to have to try ten times before I can get this right." But that acronym is less appealing.

# *Round One*
## –Answers–

1. How many months of the year start with the letter "O"? **One (1)**

2. In which sport is the term "half-nelson" used? **Wrestling**

3. On which continent is the country of Rwanda (ruh-wan-da)? **Africa**

4. Which genre of music is Randy Travis best known for performing? **Country**

5. The capital of which U.S. state is Cheyenne (shy-yan)? **Wyoming**

6. In 1963, which sport did surfer and skateboarder Tom Sims help create? **Snowboarding (the first board was built in New Jersey)**

7. From 1995 to 2015, who played the character M in the "James Bond" movies? **Judi Dench**

8. Which active comic strip was created by Jim Davis? **Garfield**

9. Which Internet security acronym stands for "completely automated public Turing Test to tell computers and humans apart"? **CAPTCHA**

10. How many years is a lustre (pronounced luster)? **Five (5) years**

    **Bonus Question** Who was the first *SNL* cast member who was born after the show premiered? **Keenan Thompson**

# Puzzle Round

Unscramble the anagrammed book titles.

1. Betrays That Egg _____

2. Treachery Chin Teeth _____

3. Threefold Foils _____

4. A Pace Wander _____

5. Barren Lewd Vow _____

6. Heathen Muggers _____

7. Vindicated Echo _____

8. Greased Toffy Fishy _____

9. Kickball Digit Moron _____

10. Jaundiced Red Piper _____

Trivia Tip: One of the best ways to solve anagrams is by finding common prefixes or suffixes. Prefixes like un- and up- are common in many words and will help by narrowing down the number of remaining letters to unscramble.

**TEAM NAME**

_____

**SCORE**

_____

# Puzzle Round
## –Answers–

Unscramble the anagrammed book titles.

Now is the time for honesty. It's OK, no one can hear us. Most of this list is classic literature or cultural phenomena and worthy of your attention. How many have you read? Probably not very many. You should. At least check out the plot summaries on their Wikipedia pages. It will make you sound smart.

1.  Betrays That Egg          **The Great Gatsby**

2.  Treachery Chin Teeth      **The Catcher In the Rye**

3.  Threefold Foils           **Lord of the Flies**

4.  A Pace Wander             **War and Peace**

5.  Barren Lewd Vow           **Brave New World**

6.  Heathen Muggers           **The Hunger Games**

7.  Vindicated Echo           **The Da Vinci Code**

8.  Greased Toffy Fishy       **Fifty Shades of Grey**

9.  Kickball Digit Moron      **To Kill a Mockingbird**

10. Jaundiced Red Piper       **Pride and Prejudice**

# Round Two

1. What does an object have to travel faster than to produce a sonic boom?

2. Traditionally, which type of fruit are "bobbed for" on Halloween?

3. Which awards are handed out by the Academy of Motion Picture Arts and Sciences?

4. On which temperature scale does water boil at 212 degrees?

5. Watched by millions of people worldwide, which annual sporting event was first held in 1967?

6. The theme song of which movie was Aerosmith's "I Don't Want To Miss a Thing"?

7. In Indian cuisine, which type of food is described by the term "aloo"?

8. In DC Comics, which fictional city is nicknamed "The Big Apricot"?

9. The name of which German city is in the logo for Porsche?

10. As of 2017, which active MLB pitcher has the most career complete games?

**Bonus Question** Invented in 1943, which popular Mexican dish is named after chef Ignacio Anaya (Ig-na-cee-oh A-na-ya)?

**Q4** Why on earth does the U.S. use the Fahrenheit scale? It makes no sense. Freezing point is 32 degrees and boiling is 212 degrees? Why come up with those numbers? In Celsius, 0 degrees is freezing and 100 degrees is boiling. That's much better. And with that I have solved the greatest issue facing the American people today. Everything else should be easy.

# Round Two
## -Answers-

1. What does an object have to travel faster than to produce a sonic boom? **Sound**

2. Traditionally, which type of fruit are "bobbed for" on Halloween? **Apples**

3. Which awards are handed out by the Academy of Motion Picture Arts and Sciences? **Academy Awards**

   🖉 **Host Note** Oscars is also an acceptable answer.

4. On which temperature scale does water boil at 212 degrees? **Fahrenheit**

5. Watched by millions of people worldwide, which annual sporting event was first held in 1967? **Super Bowl**

   🖉 **Host Note** On January 15 following the 1966 NFL season.

6. The theme song of which movie was Aerosmith's "I Don't Want To Miss a Thing"? *Armageddon*

7. In Indian cuisine, which type of food is described by the term "aloo"? **Potatoes**

8. In DC Comics, which fictional city is nicknamed "The Big Apricot"? **Metropolis**

   🖉 **Host Note** The city where Superman lives.

9. The name of which German city is in the logo for Porsche? **Stuttgart**

10. As of 2017, which active MLB pitcher has the most career complete games? **CC Sabathia**

    🖉 **Host Note** First with thirty-eight. Bartolo Colon in second place with thirty-six.

    **Bonus Question** Invented in 1943, which popular Mexican dish is named after chef Ignacio Anaya (Ig-na-cee-oh A-na-ya)? **Nachos**

    🖉 **Host Note** Nacho was his nickname.

# Picture Round

## Name the pop star

1. _____

2. _____

3. _____

4. _____

5. _____

6. _____

7. _____

8. _____

9. _____

10. _____

The problem with picture rounds like this is that they never age well. By the time you are reading this, I am betting that a few of these people will be huge stars and a few will be gone from the public eye. (Sigh.) Such is the difficult life of a trivia writer.

**TEAM NAME**

_____

**SCORE**

_____

# Picture Round
## -Answers-

Name the pop star

Tori Kelly is the voice of Mina the Elephant in the 2016 animated movie *Sing*. Every time I watch the movie I am amazed that she is not a bigger star. Not Kelly, the elephant. She can really move.

1. **Natalie La Rose**

2. **Jessie J**

3. **Tori Kelly**

4. **Becky G**

5. **Melanie Martinez**

6. **Halsey**

7. **Bebe Rexha**

8. **Justine Skye**

9. **SIA**

10. **Kiiara**

**TEAM NAME**

**SCORE**

Want more trivia?
wedontknoweither.com   *dontknoweither*  @wdktrivia

# Round Three

1. Which business phone directory takes its name from the color of paper it's printed on?

2. In musical chairs, if there are six players, how many chairs are there?

3. The call of which type of bird is described as a "gobble" sound?

4. How many times has the United States won the FIFA Men's World Cup?

5. Which major city is served by the Narita International Airport?

6. Since 1513, the kings of which country have been called either Christian or Frederik?

7. How many times was Michael Jackson married?

8. Which type of fruit is called "fraise" (pronounced "phrase") in French?

9. During the training montage in the original *Rocky* movie, which brand of sneakers is Rocky Balboa wearing?

10. In the United Kingdom, what was the marketing name of the G. I. Joe action figure?

**Bonus Question** Latin for "We hope for better things; it shall rise from the ashes," the motto of which U.S. city is "Speramus Meliora; Resurget Cineribus" (spee-rah-mus meh-lee-or-ee-ah; ree-sir-get sin-err-ee-bus)?

**Bonus** Never has a motto been more appropriate for a city. Except for maybe Baltimore, The City That Reads.

*They don't use that one anymore?*

Yeah, I guess that makes sense.

**Q2** Five chairs, seventeen bruises, two crying children and a broken leg.

# Round Three

## -Answers-

1. Which business phone directory takes its name from the color of paper it's printed on? **Yellow Pages**

   ✏ **Host Note** The White Pages are residential listings.

2. In musical chairs, if there are six players, how many chairs are there? **Five (5)**

3. The call of which type of bird is described as a "gobble" sound? **Turkey**

4. How many times has the United States won the FIFA Men's World Cup? **Zero**

   ✏ **Host Note** Best finish third place in 1930.

5. Which major city is served by the Narita International Airport? **Tokyo**

6. Since 1513, the kings of which country have been called either Christian or Frederik? **Denmark**

   ✏ **Host Note** Since 1972 Queen Margrethe has been monarch.

7. How many times was Michael Jackson married? **Two**

   ✏ **Host Note** To Lisa Marie Presley and then Debbie Rowe.

8. Which type of fruit is called "fraise" (pronounced "phrase") in French? **Strawberry**

9. During the training montage in the original *Rocky* movie, which brand of sneakers is Rocky Balboa wearing? **Converse All-Stars (Chucks)**

10. In the United Kingdom, what was the marketing name of the G.I. Joe action figure? **Action Man**

    **Bonus Question** Latin for "We hope for better things; it shall rise from the ashes," the motto of which U.S. city is "Speramus Meliora; Resurget Cineribus" (spee-rah-mus meh-lee-or-ee-ah; ree-sir-get sin-err-ee-bus)? **Detroit, Michigan**

# Fill-in-the-Blank Round

Fill-in the character played by both actors.

1. Kate Bosworth, Amy Adams

_____

2. Anthony Hopkins, Hugh Jackman

_____

3. Sean Connery, Daniel Craig

_____

4. Sally Field, Mary Elizabeth Winstead

_____

5. Eric Bana, Mark Ruffalo

_____

6. Robert Downey, Jr., Ian McKellan

_____

7. Sean Bean, Liam Neeson

_____

8. John Wayne, Jeff Bridges

_____

9. Mel Gibson, Tom Hardy

_____

10. Jodie Foster, Julianne Moore

_____

In the current age of movie reboots and franchises, this list is almost infinite. Sherlock Holmes alone has been played by more than seventy-five actors and was awarded the title of most portrayed literary human. In addition to Downey Jr. and McKellen, he has been played by Sir Christopher Lee, Charlton Heston, Peter O'Toole, Christopher Plummer, Peter Cook, Roger Moore, John Cleese, and Benedict Cumberbatch, just to name a few of the big actors.

**TEAM NAME**

_____

**SCORE**

_____

Did you know that Mad Max's last name was Rockatansky? I feel like this is something I should have known. I should pay more attention when I am watching movies.

# Fill-in-the-Blank Round
## -Answers-

Fill-in the character played by both actors.

1. Kate Bosworth, Amy Adams
   **Lois Lane**

2. Anthony Hopkins, Hugh Jackman
   **Abraham Van Helsing**

3. Sean Connery, Daniel Craig
   **James Bond**

4. Sally Field, Mary Elizabeth Winstead
   **Mary Todd Lincoln**

5. Eric Bana, Mark Ruffalo
   **Bruce Banner/The Hulk**

6. Robert Downey Jr., Ian McKellan
   **Sherlock Holmes**

7. Sean Bean, Liam Neeson
   **Zeus**

8. John Wayne, Jeff Bridges
   **Rooster Gogburn**

9. Mel Gibson, Tom Hardy
   **Mad Max Rockatansky**

10. Jodie Foster, Julianne Moore
    **Clarice Starling**

# Round Four

1. Which U.S. state is known as the "Aloha State"?

2. Which board game includes the space "Free Parking"?

3. Which track and field event starts with a metal ball held under the jaw of the competitor?

4. In which series of books is the "Three Broomsticks Inn and Pub" found?

5. Which country includes the autonomous community of the Canary Islands?

6. Which type of buildings are studied in ecclesiology (eh-clee-see-ology)?

7. At the 2016 Olympic Games, in which sport did the United States win sixteen gold medals?

8. In the 1993 movie *Super Mario Brothers*, who played Mario?

9. What does the "T. S." stand for in writer T. S. Eliot's name?

10. In which year was the last Apollo manned mission to the Moon?

**Bonus Question** Who is the highest-paid athlete on the Forbes 2017 list of the Highest-Paid Entertainers?

**Q10** In 1885 the human race was exclusively using horses for day-to-day transportation. Less than eighty-five years later we landed on the moon. Humans are awesome.

# Round Four
## –Answers–

**Q2** Free Parking is the bane of any Monopoly player's existence. Why? Because no one uses it correctly. The reason a game goes for so long is because no one plays by the actual rules. House rules are always used. A real game of Monopoly, played by the actual rules, lasts about two hours. That still doesn't make it fun though.

1. Which U.S. state is known as the "Aloha State"? **Hawaii**

2. Which board game includes the space "Free Parking"? **Monopoly**

3. Which track and field event starts with a metal ball held under the jaw of the competitor? **Shot put**

4. In which series of books is the "Three Broomsticks Inn and Pub" found? *Harry Potter*

5. Which country includes the autonomous community of the Canary Islands? **Spain**

6. Which type of buildings are studied in ecclesiology (eh-clee-see-ology)? **Churches**

7. At the 2016 Olympic Games, in which sport did the United States win sixteen gold medals? **Swimming**

8. In the 1993 movie *Super Mario Brothers*, who played Mario? **Bob Hoskins**

9. What does the "T. S." stand for in writer T. S. Eliot's name? **Thomas Stearns**

10. In which year was the last Apollo manned mission to the Moon? **1972**

**Bonus Question** Who is the highest-paid athlete on the Forbes 2017 list of the Highest-Paid Entertainers? **Cristiano Ronaldo**

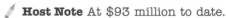 **Host Note** At $93 million to date.

# Music Round

Name the song and the artist/band.

1. I, under the pale moon, for so many years I wondered who you are/How could a person like you bring me joy?

   _____ by _____

2. She's got a competition clutch with the four on the floor/And she purrs like a kitten till the lake pipes roar

   _____ by _____

3. Who he think he is? Look at what you did to me/ Tennis shoes, don't even need to buy a new dress

   _____ by _____

4. This one, said he wants to buy you rockets/Ain't in his head, now/This one, got a princely racket/That's what I said, now

   _____ by _____

5. I put you high up in the sky/And now, you're not coming down/It slowly turned, you let me burn/And now, we're ashes on the ground

   _____ by _____

6. You come on with it, come on/You don't fight fair / That's okay, see if I care/Knock me down, it's all in vain

   _____ by _____

7. You might be a rock 'n' roll addict prancing on the stage / You might have drugs at your command, women in a cage

   _____ by _____

8. He's really down and he's no/Clown yeah yeah /He has the finest penthouse/I've even seen in town yeah, yeah

   _____ by _____

9. This love found us/Now I see it/This love up down/ Please believe

   _____ by _____

10. Thrift shop, pimp strut walking/Little bit of humble, little bit of cautious

   _____ by _____

Theme

_____

**TEAM NAME**

_____

**SCORE**

_____

Tennis: the only thing that really links Bob Dylan, Macklemore, and the Beach Boys.

# Music Round
## –Answers–

Name the song and the artist/band.

1. I, under the pale moon, for so many years I wondered who you are / How could a person like you bring me joy? **The Sign** by **Ace of Base**

2. She's got a competition clutch with the four on the floor / And she purrs like a kitten till the lake pipes roar **Little Deuce Coupe** by **Beach Boys**

3. Who he think he is? Look at what you did to me / Tennis shoes, don't even need to buy a new dress **Crazy In Love** by **Beyoncé**

4. This one, said he wants to buy you rockets / Ain't in his head, now / This one, got a princely racket / That's what I said, now **Two Princes** by **Spin Doctors**

5. I put you high up in the sky / And now, you're not coming down / It slowly turned, you let me burn/And now, we're ashes on the ground **Wrecking Ball** by **Miley Cyrus**

6. You come on with it, come on / You don't fight fair / That's okay, see if I care / Knock me down, it's all in vain **Hit Me with Your Best Shot** by **Pat Benatar**

7. You might be a rock 'n' roll addict prancing on the stage / You might have drugs at your command, women in a cage **Gotta Serve Somebody** by **Bob Dylan**

8. He's really down and he's no / Clown yeah yeah / He has the finest penthouse / I've even seen in town yeah, yeah **The Boy from New York City** by **The Ad Libs**

9. This love found us / Now I see it / This love up down/Please believe **Not Your Fault** by **AwolNation**

10. Thrift shop, pimp strut walking / Little bit of humble, little bit of cautious **Can't Hold Us** by **Macklemore (Ft. Ryan Lewis)**

Theme: **Tennis**

# Round Five

1. In the Olympics, what color medal is awarded for second place?

2. In the Christmas song, which type of animal is Rudolph?

3. On the national flag of Japan, what color is the circle?

4. In Greek mythology, to what did Icarus fly too close?

5. Which type of orchard is named in the title of a play by Anton Chekhov (Check-ov)?

6. Launched in 1971, which planet did the Mariner 9 space probe study?

7. Which former *American Idol* contestant has performed as the lead singer of Queen?

8. In which sport is "warding off" a foul?

9. The name of which river means "waterfalls" in the Sotho language?

10. What is an object shaped like if it is described as "ichthyomorphic" (ick-thee-yo-more-fick)?

**Bonus Question** In the 1933 Marx Brothers movie *Duck Soup*, what was the name of the country headed by Groucho Marx?

**Q1** Did you ever notice that the guy in second place on the podium always looks pissed while the guy in third always looks happy? I guess that the difference between, "I was so close to being the best" and "Man, I am just happy to be up here."

# Round Five
## –Answers–

1. In the Olympics, what color medal is awarded for second place? **Silver**

2. In the Christmas song, which type of animal is Rudolph? **Reindeer (red-nosed)**

3. On the national flag of Japan, what color is the circle? **Red**

4. In Greek mythology, to what did Icarus fly too close? **The sun**

5. Which type of orchard is named in the title of a play by Anton Chekhov (Check-ov)? **Cherry**

   **Host Note** The title of the play is *The Cherry Orchard*.

6. Launched in 1971, which planet did the Mariner 9 space probe study? **Mars**

7. Which former *American Idol* contestant has performed as the lead singer of Queen? **Adam Lambert**

8. In which sport is "warding off" a foul? **Lacrosse**

9. The name of which river means "waterfalls" in the Sotho language? **Limpopo**

   **Host Note** In central southern Africa.

10. What is an object shaped like if it is described as "ichthyomorphic" (ick-thee-yo-more-fick)? **Fish**

    **Bonus Question** In the 1933 Marx Brothers movie *Duck Soup*, what was the name of the country headed by Groucho Marx? **Freedonia**

# GAME SEVEN

"The fellow who thinks he knows it all is especially annoying
to those of us who do."

—Harold Coffin

HAT IS THE CAPITOL OF MARYLAND WHO INVENTED
THE NAME WE THE ACTIOR THAT PLAYS INDIA
L DONT WROTE A MUSICALBASED ON THE LIFE OF WH
FATHER WHICH COMPANY MAKES THE IPAD EITHER
JUICE TO MAKE A SCREW DRIVER WHICH TWO NFL T
EW YORK HOW MANY ELEMENTS ARE ON THE PERIO
MAMBO NO 5 WHAT IS THE WESTERN MOST STAT
TES WHO WROTE THE HARRY POTTER SERIES WHAT
ACK OF THE 5 DOLLAR BILL WHAT DOES AOL STAND F
ANY MEMBERS OF THE PUSSYCAT DOLLS HOW OLD
WHICH YEAR DID HENRY FORD INVENT THE MODE
INK WAS CREATED AT THE UNIVERSITY OF FLORIDA
AD ALL OF THESE QUESTIONS WHAT ARE YOU DOING W
ANY TRIVIA WRITERS DOES IT TAKE TO CHANGE A L
IE BOSTON MARATHON WHAT IS THE MOST VIEWED
WHICH NETWORK HAS THE EXCLUSIVE TRIVIA TO
HOW MUCH DID A 30 SECOND NIGHT IN THE SUPERB
K IS IN THE DONE BY THE WINNER OF THE INDIANAP
IS THE GREATEST MOVIE OF ALL TIME HOW MANY EY
PLAYING CARDS WHO SHOT JR WHEN IS THE IDES
THE NAME OF THE LEADER OF NORTH KOREA WHAT
RING MARCH MADNESS WHEN WAS THE CONSTITU TIO
NCH OF GOVERNMENT IS LEAD BY THE SUPREME C
S DOES IT TAKE TO GET TO THE CENTER OF A TO
HE CITY TRIVIA HEADQUARTERS WHAT DO YOU GET
W AND BLUE WHO LIVES IN THE PINEAPPLE UNDER
THE NAME OF THE FIRST PRESIDENT OF THE UNITED
HAT WAS THE FIRST MAND MADE OBJECT TO BREAK T
HAT IS THE CAPITOL OF MARYLAND WHO INVENTED
HE NAME WE THE ACTIOR THAT PLAYS INDIA
DONT WROTE A MUSICALBASED ON THE LIFE OF W

# Round One

1. What is the result of ten quadrupled?

2. Which organ is stimulated by a pacemaker?

3. In which sport is Lou Gehrig a Hall of Fame player?

4. In which decade were the first two *Godfather* movies released?

5. Which fruit juice is included in the recipe for a Blue Hawaiian cocktail?

6. Which actor launched the charity website SixDegrees.org?

7. In the *Lord of the Rings* series, what is the name Sam short for?

8. Which Old Testament prophet had a wife named Zipporah?

9. If an athlete wears the initials "KSA," which country are they representing?

10. In which English county is Stonehenge?

    **Bonus Question** In 1963, which fad item was invented by British accountant Edward Craven-Walker?

**Q3** While not appropriate in any way, the Medical Hall of Fame is not a correct answer. It is a common answer, but not correct.

**Q4** First two? There are only two.

*But what about...*

There were only two.

# Round One
## –Answers–

1. What is the result of ten quadrupled? **Forty (40)**

2. Which organ is stimulated by a pacemaker? **Heart**

3. In which sport is Lou Gehrig a Hall of Fame player? **Baseball**

4. In which decade were the first two *Godfather* movies released? **1970s**

5. Which fruit juice is included in the recipe for a Blue Hawaiian cocktail? **Pineapple juice**

6. Which actor launched the charity website SixDegrees. org? **Kevin Bacon**

7. In the *Lord of the Rings* series, what is the name Sam short for? **Samwise**

8. Which Old Testament prophet had a wife named Zipporah? **Moses**

9. If an athlete wears the initials "KSA," which country are they representing? **Saudi Arabia**

   **Host Note** The initials stand for "Kingdom of Saudi Arabia."

10. In which English county is Stonehenge? **Wiltshire**

    **Bonus Question** In 1963, which fad item was invented by British accountant Edward Craven-Walker? **Lava lamp (or Astro lamp)**

# Puzzle Round

Match the ridiculous National Day to the
month in which it occurs.

_____ 1. National Polar
     Bear Day

A. January

_____ 2. National
     Frankenstein Day

B. February

_____ 3. National
     Kazoo Day

C. March

_____ 4. National
     Hamburger Day

D. April

_____ 5. National Talk
     Like a Pirate Day

E. May

_____ 6. National Underwear
     Day

F. June

_____ 7. National Lemon
     Chiffon Cake Day

G. July

_____ 8. National Bugs
     Bunny Day

H. August

_____ 9. National Chili
     Dogs Day

I. September

_____ 10. National
     Sunglasses Day

J. October

There is a national
day for everything.
It is starting to get
ridiculous. I mean
I can get behind
Bugs Bunny day
or Hamburger
day, but National
Underwear Day? We
need to stop letting
people make things
like this official.
Otherwise we will
end up with Boaty
McBoatface Day.

**TEAM NAME**

_____

**SCORE**

_____

I get why Polar
Bear Day is in
February and
Sunglasses Day is
in June, but why on
earth is Kazoo Day
in January? What
tie can there be
between Kazoos and
January? Is it a cold
weather instrument?

# Puzzle Round
## –Answers–

Match the ridiculous National Day to the
month in which it occurs.

**B** 1. National Polar
Bear Day

A. January

**J** 2. National
Frankenstein Day

B. February

**A** 3. National
Kazoo Day

C. March

**E** 4. National
Hamburger Day

D. April

**I** 5. National Talk
Like a Pirate Day

E. May

**H** 6. National Underwear
Day

F. June

**C** 7. National Lemon
Chiffon Cake Day

G. July

**D** 8. National Bugs
Bunny Day

H. August

**G** 9. National Chili
Dogs Day

I. September

**F** 10. National
Sunglasses Day

J. October

Want more trivia?
wedontknoweither.com  ⬤ ⬤ dontknoweither  ⬤ @wdketrivia

# Round Two

1. Somebody who becomes angry or irritated is said to be "hot under the..." what?

2. What term describes the fastest gait of a horse?

3. Which continent does the Danube (Dan-youb) River flow through?

4. Which cartoon series included the characters Cheetara, Panthro, and Lion-O?

5. What has been removed from a "deplumed" bird?

6. In which country was cyclist Alberto Contador born?

7. Which German word translates as "good health"?

8. What is the term for the knob at the end of a sword hilt?

9. Which computer company was co-founded by Ronald Wayne?

10. Who won an Academy Award, a Screen Actors Guild Award, and a Golden Globe for her 2006 portrayal of Queen Elizabeth II?

   **Bonus Question** Which sport combines elements of basketball and polo and is the national sport of Argentina?

**Q2** Fun fact: the average horse can produce 1 horsepower over a sustained period of time. Weird how stuff like that works out.

**Q9** Is it weird that most people have heard of Steve Wozniak and everyone has heard of Steve Jobs, but few know who Ronald Wayne is? It would suck to be the guy who invented Apple that no one knows. Not as much as it would suck to have invented Apple and been paid $800 bucks for it, which is what happened, but sucks nonetheless.

# Round Two
## –Answers–

1. Somebody who becomes angry or irritated is said to be "hot under the..." what? **Collar**

2. What term describes the fastest gait of a horse? **Gallop**

   ✎ **Host Note** A gallop pace averages twenty to thirty miles per hour.

3. Which continent does the Danube (Dan-youb) River flow through? **Europe**

4. Which cartoon series included the characters Cheetara, Panthro, and Lion-O? **Thundercats**

5. What has been removed from a "deplumed" bird? **Feathers**

6. In which country was cyclist Alberto Contador born? **Spanish**

7. Which German word translates as "good health"? **Gesundheit**

8. What is the term for the knob at the end of a sword hilt? **Pommel**

9. Which computer company was co-founded by Ronald Wayne? **Apple**

   ✎ **Host Note** It was co-founded with Steve Jobs and Steve Wozniak.

10. Who won an Academy Award, a Screen Actors Guild Award, and a Golden Globe for her 2006 portrayal of Queen Elizabeth II? **Helen Mirren**

    **Bonus Question** Which sport combines elements of basketball and polo and is the national sport of Argentina? **Pato**

# Picture Round

## Princes: Name the Movie

1. _____

2. _____

3. _____

4. _____

5. _____

6. _____

7. _____

8. _____

9. _____

10. _____

I have always wanted to be royalty. Do you think that there is some country out there that has a daughter of marriageable age that is available for a lowly trivia writer? If you are that daughter, or if you know one, hit me up?

**TEAM NAME**

_____

**SCORE**

_____

# Picture Round
## -Answers-

Princes: Name the Movie

Why are princes in movies always ridiculously good looking or terribly repulsive? Why don't they ever show a regular guy as a prince? This is why King Ralph will always be the standard for royal beauty in film.

1.  **Little Prince**

2.  **Space balls**
    (Prince Valium)

3.  **Coming to America**
    (Prince Akeem)

4.  **Princess Bride**
    (Prince Humperdinck)

5.  **Purple Rain**
    (Prince)

6.  **Enchanted**
    (Prince Edward)

7.  **Your Highness**
    (Prince Thadeous)

8.  **Mirror Mirror**
    (Prince Alcott)

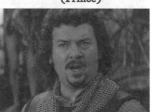

9.  **Braveheart**
    (Prince Edward)

10. **Ever After**
    (Prince Henry)

**TEAM NAME**

**SCORE**

Want more trivia?
wedontknoweither.com  *dontknoweither*  @wdketrivia

# Round Three

1. Which type of reptile is a python?

2. Which basic color comes in shades of burgundy and carmine?

3. Which *Indiana Jones* movie is primarily set in India?

4. Who wrote the plays *The Crucible* and *Death of a Salesman*?

5. Which former Texas A&M quarterback is nicknamed "Johnny Football"?

6. Which novel turned movie ends with the line: "I'm so glad to be home again"?

7. Which U.S. state was the site of the first atomic bomb test?

8. The protagonist of which novel is a fireman named Guy Montag?

9. In which U.S. Civil War battle was Pickett's Charge?

10. Within a range of two, how many feathers are on an Olympic Badminton shuttlecock (birdie)?

**Bonus Question** The largest island park in the United States, which city is home to 987-acre Belle Isle Park?

**Q3** Did you know that they are making a fourth Indiana Jones movie? It is currently untitled and set to come out in 2020.

*But that isn't the fourth movie, it is the...*

(Sigh.) Didn't we already cover this like six pages ago with the *Godfather* question? This is the fourth movie.

**Q4** A far greater accomplishment was to be married to Marilyn Monroe looking like he did. Wordsmith indeed.

# Round Three
## -Answers-

1. Which type of reptile is a python? **Snake**

2. Which basic color comes in shades of burgundy and carmine? **Red**

3. Which *Indiana Jones* movie is primarily set in India? ***Indiana Jones and the Temple of Doom***

4. Who wrote the plays *The Crucible* and *Death of a Salesman*? **Arthur Miller**

5. Which former Texas A&M quarterback is nicknamed "Johnny Football"? **Johnny Manziel**

6. Which novel turned movie ends with the line "I'm so glad to be home again"? ***The Wonderful Wizard of Oz***

7. Which U.S. state was the site of the first atomic bomb test? **New Mexico**

8. The protagonist of which novel is a fireman named Guy Montag? **Fahrenheit 451**

9. In which U.S. Civil War battle was Pickett's Charge? **Battle of Gettysburg**

10. Within a range of two, how many feathers are on an Olympic Badminton shuttlecock (birdie)? **Sixteen (16)**

    **Host Note** The answers fourteen to eighteen (14–18) are also acceptable.

    **Bonus Question** The largest island park in the United States, which city is home to 987-acre Belle Isle Park? **Detroit, MI**

# Fill-in-the-Blank Round

Fill-in the last ten NBA Finals MVP's.

1. 2018 _____

2. 2017 _____

3. 2016 _____

4. 2015 _____

5. 2014 _____

6. 2013 _____

7. 2012 _____

8. 2011 _____

9. 2010 _____

10. 2009 _____

Did you know: Of the top 50 most watched sporting events in 2016, Game 7 of the NBA Championship was the only basketball game. The NFL took 9 of the top 10 spots. Game 7 of the World Series that year came in at number 5. The Winter Olympics even made a few appearances on the list. My point here is that no one watches hockey.

**TEAM NAME**

_____

**SCORE**

_____

# *Fill-in-the-Blank Round*
## -Answers-

Fill-in the last ten NBA Finals MVP's.

OK time to begin the ultimate NBA debate. Who was the greatest of all time? Well in the last ten years it seems that Kobe won two MVPs and Lebron has won more.

*That seems to make it a pretty obvious choice.*

*It's Jordan.*

*Yep. Glad we both agree on that one.*

1.  2018     Kevin Durant

2.  2017     Kevin Durant

3.  2016     Lebron James

4.  2015     Andre Iguodala

5.  2014     Kawhi Leonard

6.  2013     Lebron James

7.  2012     Lebron James

8.  2011     Dirk Nowitzki

9.  2010     Kobe Bryant

10. 2009     Kobe Bryant

# Round Four

1. What does the L stand for in the text abbreviation "ROFL"?

2. Which liquid measurement is abbreviated as "pt"?

3. What is the collective name of the lakes that include Lake Superior and Lake Ontario?

4. Which country is the setting of the 1964 musical *Fiddler on the Roof*?

5. What is the call sign of a U.S. Marine Corps aircraft carrying the President of the United States?

6. Which form of Buddhism is also known by the Chinese name "Chan"?

7. The mascot of the 1980 Summer Olympics in Moscow, which type of animal was Mischa?

8. After oxygen, which is the most abundant element in the Earth's crust?

9. What was Steven Spielberg's first theatrical release war movie?

10. In which country was Ernő Rubik, inventor of the Rubik's Cube, born?

**Bonus Question** Which movie was nominated for the most Academy Awards without winning Best Picture?

**Q1** Has anyone in the history of the world actually texted ROFL while actually ROFL? Same question for LOL. Also, why don't we have an abbreviation for mildly amused snicker? Seems like we would use that more often.

**Q7** Wow...the mascot of the Russian Olympics was a bear. How is that a 7-point question? That's it, throw out the whole book. We need a rewrite.

1. What does the L stand for in the text abbreviation "ROFL"? **Laughing**

   ✏ **Host Note** The entire abbreviation stands for "Rolling On Floor Laughing."

2. Which liquid measurement is abbreviated as "pt"? **Pint**

3. What is the collective name of the lakes that include Lake Superior and Lake Ontario? **The Great Lakes**

4. Which country is the setting of the 1964 musical *Fiddler on the Roof*? **Russia**

5. What is the call sign of a U.S. Marine Corps aircraft carrying the President of the United States? **Marine One**

6. Which form of Buddhism is also known by the Chinese name "Chan"? **Zen**

7. The mascot of the 1980 Summer Olympics in Moscow, which type of animal was Mischa? **Bear**

8. After oxygen, which is the most abundant element in the Earth's crust? **Silicon**

9. What was Steven Spielberg's first theatrical release war movie? ***1941***

10. In which country was Ernő Rubik, inventor of the Rubik's Cube, born? **Hungary**

    **Bonus Question** Which movie was nominated for the most Academy Awards without winning Best Picture? **La La land**

    ✏ **Host Note** It had fourteen nominations and won six of them.

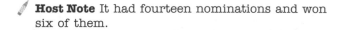

# Music Round

Name the song and the artist/band.

1. Your body is banging mama, but where your brains at? / I'm still the same cat when I was younger running with Bad Boys

   _____ by _____

2. With a gattle in her bud to get a little wild / Pony-tail and a pretty smile / Rope me in from a country mile

   _____ by _____

3. And that's what they don't see mmm mmm / I'm dancing on my own / I'll make the moves up as I go

   _____ by _____

4. Trick, what's happenin' let 'em see, show the world / Attention all y'all blazin' pimps / Right now in the place to be

   _____ by _____

5. And every demon wants his pound of flesh / But I like to keep some things to myself

   _____ by _____

6. I want everybody in the house to know / I came here tonight to hear the crowd go

   _____ by _____

7. Groovin' loose heart to heart / We put in motion every single part / Funky sounds wall to wall/We're bumpin' booties, havin' us a ball

   _____ by _____

8. I don't know where I'm gonna go / Don't know what I'm gonna do / Must be somebody up above saying come on Brittany

   _____ by _____

9. I like the way you comb your hair (uh!) / I like the stylish clothes you wear (uh!)

   _____ by _____

10. Ey (ey) / Ey (ey) / Ey (ey) / Ey (ey) /
    _Con los terroristas_

    _____ by _____

Theme _____

**Q3** And that's what they don't know mmm mmm, that's what they don't know mmm mmm. But I keep cruising, can't stop, won't stop grooving. It's like I got this music in my mind saying it's gonna be alright... sorry, got carried away there. That song's my jam.

**TEAM NAME**

_____

**SCORE**

_____

OK, it doesn't seem really fair that they threw the "Harlem Shake" in there. Those aren't even words. How are you supposed to get that? I would demand a refund if I were you... not for this book. That would cost me money. Go to a Target or something. Demand a refund from them.

*But that doesn't make any sense.*

Exactly. They will never see it coming.

# Music Round
## –Answers–

Name the song and the artist/band.

1. Your body is banging mama, but where your brains at? / I'm still the same cat when I was younger running with Bad Boys **Shake Ya Tail Feather** by **Nelly, Murphy Lee, and P. Diddy**

2. With a gattle in her bud to get a little wild / Ponytail and a pretty smile / Rope me in from a country mile **Country Girl (Shake It for Me)** by **Luke Bryan**

3. And that's what they don't see mmm mmm / I'm dancing on my own / I'll make the moves up as I go **Shake It Off** by **Taylor Swift**

4. Trick, what's happenin' let 'em see, show the world / Attention all y'all blazin' pimps / Right now in the place to be **Shake It Fast** by **Mystikal**

5. And every demon wants his pound of flesh / But I like to keep some things to myself **Shake It Out** by **Florence + The Machine**

6. I want everybody in the house to know / I came here tonight to hear the crowd go **Boom! Shake the Room** by **DJ Jazzy Jeff and Fresh Prince**

7. Groovin' loose heart to heart / We put in motion every single part / Funky sounds wall to wall / We're bumpin' booties, havin' us a ball **Shake Your Groove Thing** by **Peaches and Herb**

8. I don't know where I'm gonna go / Don't know what I'm gonna do / Must be somebody up above saying come on Brittany **Hold On** by **Alabama Shakes**

9. I like the way you comb your hair (uh!) / I like the stylish clothes you wear (uh!) **Rump Shaker** by **Wreck-X-N-Effect**

10. Ey (ey) / Ey (ey) / Ey (ey) / Ey (ey) / *Con los terroristas* **Harlem Shake** by **Baauer**

Theme: **Shake**

Want more trivia? wedontknoweither.com   dontknoweither   @wdketrivia

# Round Five

1. As of 2018, from the viewer's perspective, which way does the peacock in the NBC logo face?

2. What is the term for someone who uses each hand equally well?

3. Which actress's first biological child is named Shiloh Nouvel?

4. In which sport are épées (eh-pay) and foils used?

5. In the original version of Trivial Pursuit, which subject goes with Science in the green category?

6. From which country are the pop groups "Ace of Base" and "Roxette"?

7. Which type of animal is a whinchat?

8. On the television show *Seinfeld*, what was George Costanza's job title for the New York Yankees?

9. Which mountain range includes the active volcano with the highest elevation?

10. How many of the *James Bond* theme songs have hit number one on the Billboard Hot 100?

**Bonus Question** Who was the first actor to appear on the cover of *TIME* magazine?

**Q1** Is it the left or the right? Or wait... is it straight on? What are the colors of the peacocks feathers? How many feathers does it have? Has it always had that many feathers? When did NBC start using the peacock as a logo? What was the first television network? Who invented the television? Greatest inventions of all time? And thus I have killed an hour on Wikipedia doing nothing but clicking links. The Information Age is cool.

**Q5** Trivia Night Tip: Most trivia nights at bars everywhere in the country are run by either the guy who owns the bar or someone who is doing it for the free drinks. As a result, there isn't too much effort going into the creation of the questions. If you go to Amazon and type in "Trivial Pursuit" and buy the first game that pops up, you are very likely to get the same questions mailed to your door that they are asking at the bar...unless they are using this book...in which case you already have the teachers edition for tonight's trivia...at least try and make it look close...we don't want to piss off too many people.

# Round Five
## –Answers–

1. As of 2018, from the viewer's perspective, which way does the peacock in the NBC logo face? **Right**

    *Host Note* The original logo faced left.

2. What is the term for someone who uses each hand equally well? **Ambidextrous**

3. Which actress' first biological child is named Shiloh Nouvel? **Angelina Jolie**

4. In which sport are épées (eh-pay) and foils used? **Fencing**

5. In the original version of Trivial Pursuit, which subject goes with Science in the green category? **Nature**

6. From which country are the pop groups Ace of Base and Roxette? **Sweden**

7. Which type of animal is a whinchat? **Bird**

8. On the television show *Seinfeld*, what was George Costanza's job title for the New York Yankees? **Assistant to the Traveling Secretary**

9. Which mountain range includes the active volcano with the highest elevation? **Andes**

    *Host Note* The stratovolcano is the Ojos del Salado.

10. How many of the *James Bond* theme songs have hit number one on the Billboard Hot 100? **One (1)**

    *Host Note* It was "A View to a Kill" by Duran Duran.

    **Bonus Question** Who was the first actor to appear on the cover of *TIME* magazine? **Charlie Chaplin**

    *Host Note* On July 6, 1925.

# GAME EIGHT

"One never realizes how much and how little
he knows until he starts talking."

—Louis L'Amour

HAT IS THE CAPITOL OF MARYLAND WHO INVENTED
HE NAME WE THE ACTIOR THAT PLAYS INDIA
L DONT WROTE A MUSICALBASED ON THE LIFE OF WF
FATHER WHICH COMPANY MAKES THE IPAD EITHER
JUICE TO MAKE A SCREW DRIVER WHICH TWO NFL T
EW YORK HOW MANY ELEMENTS ARE ON THE PERIO
MAMBO NO 5 WHAT IS THE WESTERN MOST STAT
TES WHO WROTE THE HARRY POTTER SERIES WHAT
ACK OF THE 5 DOLLAR BILL WHAT DOES AOL STAND
IANY MEMBERS OF THE PUSSYCAT DOLLS HOW OLD
WHICH YEAR DID HENRY FORD INVENT THE MODE
INK WAS CREATED AT THE UNIVERSITY OF FLORID
AD ALL OF THESE QUESTIONS WHAT ARE YOU DOING
IANY TRIVIA WRITERS DOES IT TAKE TO CHANGE A I
HE BOSTON MARATHON WHAT IS THE MOST VIEWED
VHICH NETWORK HAS THE EXCLUSIVE TRIVIA TO
IOW MUCH DID A 30 SECOND NIGHT IN THE SUPERF
K IS IN THE DONE BY THE WINNER OF THE INDIANAP
IS THE GREATEST MOVIE OF ALL TIME HOW MANY EY
PLAYING CARDS WHO SHOT JR WHEN IS THE IDES
THE NAME OF THE LEADER OF NORTH KOREA WHAT
RING MARCH MADNESS WHEN WAS THE CONSTITU TI
NCH OF GOVERNMENT IS LEAD BY THE SUPREME C
S DOES IT TAKE TO GET TO THE CENTER OF A TO
HE CITY TRIVIA HEADQUARTERS WHAT DO YOU GET
W AND BLUE WHO LIVES IN THE PINEAPPLE UNDEF
THE NAME OF THE FIRST PRESIDENT OF THE UNITED
HAT WAS THE FIRST MAND MADE OBJECT TO BREAK T
HAT IS THE CAPITOL OF MARYLAND WHO INVENTED
HE NAME WE THE ACTIOR THAT PLAYS INDIA
L DONT WROTE A MUSICALBASED ON THE LIFE OF WF

# Round One

1. How many sides does a parallelogram have?

2. Which of a parent's children is referred to as primogeniture (pry-muh-jen-eh-cher)?

3. Which branch of physics studies forces acting on objects moving through air?

4. The accessory fruits of which common garden flower are called "hips"?

5. Winning seven games in 1995, which NFL (National Football League) team set the record for most wins by an expansion team during its first season?

6. Who was the first NASA astronaut to travel into space?

7. Since 1897, in which U.S. city is the world's oldest annual marathon held?

8. In the original logo for Saab automobiles, what color is the griffin's head?

9. What is the term for the loose fold of skin on the neck of an old person?

10. After which Nobel prize-winning physicist is the official International System (SI) Unit for radioactivity named?

**Bonus Question** The mascot of the 2014 FIFA World Cup, which type of animal was Fuleco (foo-lay-co)?

**Q6** Look closely... we are asking for the first astronaut... not the first person. Semantics matter. Especially at trivia night.

**Q7** The runner up in the female division of the 2018 Boston Marathon was not immediately given credit for her accomplishment. You see, runners are a tight knit group and everyone with a real chance at winning is known well before the race even starts. This woman was racing in her second marathon ever. Needless to say, when she finished race officials were skeptical. They had to go back and check her GPS to make sure she didn't cheat. She didn't and was given her well-deserved accolade. This story gives me hope. Maybe one day I will get out of my comfy office chair and do something with my life...yea... probably not.

# Round One
## –Answers–

1. How many sides does a parallelogram have?
   **Four (4)**

2. Which of a parent's children is referred to as primogeniture (pry-muh-jen-eh-cher)? **First born**

3. Which branch of physics studies forces acting on objects moving through air? **Aerodynamics**

4. The accessory fruits of which common garden flower are called "hips"? **Rose**

5. Winning seven games in 1995, which NFL (National Football League) team set the record for most wins by an expansion team during its first season? **Carolina Panthers**

6. Who was the first NASA astronaut to travel into space? **Alan Shepard**

7. Since 1897, in which U.S. city is the world's oldest annual marathon held? **Boston**

8. In the original logo for Saab automobiles, what color is the griffin's head? **Red**

9. What is the term for the loose fold of skin on the neck of an old person? **Dewlap**

10. After which Nobel prize-winning physicist is the official International System (SI) Unit  for radioactivity named?  **Henri Becquerel**

    **Host Note** The Curie is non-SI and used mostly in the U.S.

    **Bonus Question** The mascot of the 2014 FIFA World Cup, which type of animal was Fuleco (foo-lay-co)? **Armadillo**

# Puzzle Round

Match the author to their lesser known work.

_____ 1. JRR Tolkien

_____ 2. George Orwell

_____ 3. John Steinbeck

_____ 4. Mark Twain

_____ 5. John Updike

_____ 6. Ernest Hemingway

_____ 7. William Faulkner

_____ 8. JK Rowling

_____ 9. Phillip K Dick

_____ 10. RL Stine

A. *Flow my tears, the policeman said*

B. *The Silmarillion*

C. *Pudd'nhead Wilson*

D. *The Witches of Eastwick*

E. *The Casual Vacancy*

F. *As I Lay Dying*

G. *When Good Ghouls Go Bad*

H. *Men Without Women*

I. *Coming Up for Air*

J. *The Acts of King Arthur and His Noble Knights*

In my opinion, there are no lesser works. Books are hard to write and each one is an accomplishment.

*Even this one?*

(Sigh)...I hate you.

**TEAM NAME**

_____

**SCORE**

_____

# Puzzle Round
## –Answers–

Match the author to their lesser known work.

Can Tolkien's *Silmarillion* be considered a lesser known work at this point? I guess our new definition is, "If it makes less than 5 billion at the box office it is lesser known." So it is written, so it shall be.

**B** 1. JRR Tolkien

A. *Flow my tears, the policeman said*

**I** 2. George Orwell

B. *The Silmarillion*

**J** 3. John Steinbeck

C. *Pudd'nhead Wilson*

**C** 4. Mark Twain

D. *The Witches of Eastwick*

**D** 5. John Updike

E. *The Casual Vacancy*

**H** 6. Ernest Hemingway

F. *As I Lay Dying*

**F** 7. William Faulkner

G. *When Good Ghouls Go Bad*

**E** 8. JK Rowling

H. *Men Without Women*

**A** 9. Phillip K Dick

I. *Coming Up for Air*

**G** 10. RL Stine

J. *The Acts of King Arthur and His Noble Knights*

**TEAM NAME**

**SCORE**

# Round Two

1. How many days are in ten weeks?

2. What number first appeared on Heinz products in 1896?

3. The child of an individual's first cousin is known as their "first cousin once" what?

4. In Norse mythology, where are the souls of warriors that die a heroic death?

5. What was the last name of the lead family on *The Cosby Show*?

6. Which fruit flavor is Cointreau (Kwon-troh) liquor?

7. Which lake borders both Uganda and Kenya?

8. In which decade was the Wimbledon Tennis Tournament first held?

9. The death of which leader was the subject of the Walt Whitman poem "O Captain! My Captain!"?

10. Which part of a building may be described as a "mansard"?

**Bonus Question** In 2011, which shoe company launched the Brooklyn-based recording studio "Rubber Tracks"?

**Q10** So, I was a general contractor for twelve years and built million-dollar houses in Washington, D.C. and I have no idea what the answer is. Good Luck!

**Q7** If there is a question about a body of water in Africa. The answer is Lake Victoria. 100 percent.

# Round Two
## -Answers-

1. How many days are in ten weeks? **Seventy (70)**

2. What number first appeared on Heinz products in 1896? **57**

3. The child of an individual's first cousin is known as their "first cousin once" what? **Removed**

4. In Norse mythology, where are the souls of warriors that die a heroic death? **Valhalla**

5. What was the last name of the lead family on *The Cosby Show*? **Huxtable**

6. Which fruit flavor is Cointreau (Kwon-troh) liquor? **Orange**

7. Which lake borders both Uganda and Kenya? **Lake Victoria**

8. In which decade was the Wimbledon Tennis Tournament first held? **1870s**

   🖉 **Host Note** Specifically 1877.

9. The death of which leader was the subject of the Walt Whitman poem "O Captain! My Captain!"? **Abraham Lincoln**

10. Which part of a building may be described as a "mansard"? **Roof**

    **Bonus Question** In 2011, which shoe company launched the Brooklyn-based recording studio "Rubber Tracks"? **Converse**

# *Picture Round*

### Fictional Houses: Name the Resident(s)

1. _____

2. _____

3. _____

4. _____

5. _____

6. _____

7. _____

8. _____

9. _____

10. _____

If you had to choose which one of these houses to live in, which one would it be? Not the world or the circumstances, just the house.

**TEAM NAME**

_____

**SCORE**

_____

I would probably pick Winnie the Pooh's house. There is something appealing to me about living in a house with an unlimited honey supply. Just think of all the things you could do with that honey?

Are you thinking about it?

You went sexual real fast didn't you? You're dirty.

**TEAM NAME**

_____

**SCORE**

_____

# Picture Round
## -Answers-

Fictional Houses: Name the Resident(s)

1. **The Weasley's**
(Harry Potter)

2. **Winnie The Pooh**

3. **Carl Fredrickson**
(Up)

4. **Tony Montana**
(Scarface)

5. **Bilbo Baggins**
(Lord of the Rings)

6. **Jay Gatsby**
(The Great Gatsby)

7. **Tony Stark**
(Scarface)

8. **Bruce Wayne**
(Gotham)

9. **Squidward**
(Spongebob Squarepants)

10. **The Simpsons**

Want more trivia?
wedontknoweither.com  dontknoweither  @wdketrivia

# Round Three

1. When cartoon characters have a good idea, what usually appears above their heads?

2. Another term for natural selection is "survival of the..." what?

3. Which chemical element do anemic persons usually lack in their blood?

4. In the name of the television show, what is "O.C." short for?

5. What is the official language of Egypt?

6. In track and field, what is the term for the first part of a triple jump?

7. How many different herbs are listed in the Simon & Garfunkel song "Scarborough Fair"?

8. Cruciate (crew-she-ate) ligaments are arranged similar to which letter of the alphabet?

9. What was the prequel to the 1998 movie *U.S. Marshals*?

10. What does the name of the Irish capital "Dublin" translate to in English?

**Bonus Question** Which city is home to the first zoo in the U.S.?

**Q9** What ever happened to Wesley Snipes? I know he had tax problems, but that means he should be working more, not less, right?

# Round Three
## -Answers-

1. When cartoon characters have a good idea, what usually appears above their heads? **Light bulb**

2. Another term for natural selection is "survival of the..." what? **Fittest**

3. Which chemical element do anemic persons usually lack in their blood? **Iron**

4. In the name of the television show, what is "O.C." short for? **Orange County**

5. What is the official language of Egypt? **Arabic**

6. In track and field, what is the term for the first part of a triple jump? **Hop**

    **Host Note** Hop-skip-jump.

7. How many different herbs are listed in the Simon & Garfunkel song "Scarborough Fair"? **Four (4)**

    **Host Note** The are: parsley, sage, rosemary, and thyme.

8. Cruciate (crew-she-ate) ligaments are arranged similar to which letter of the alphabet? **X**

    **Host Note** Cruciate means cross-shaped.

9. What was the prequel to the 1998 movie *U.S. Marshals*? **The Fugitive**

10. What does the name of the Irish capital "Dublin" translate to in English? **Black/dark pool**

    **Bonus Question** Which city is home to the first zoo in the U.S.? **Philadelphia, PA**

# Fill-in-the-Blank Round

Fill-in the body of water in which the island is located.

1. Aruba _____

2. Tonga _____

3. Cyprus _____

4. Guernsey _____

5. Bahrain _____

6. Mauritius _____

7. Lesbos _____

8. The Isle of Man _____

9. Krakatoa _____

10. Three Mile Island _____

Are these all real? I'm pretty sure Krakatoa isn't a real word.

**TEAM NAME**

_____

**SCORE**

# Fill-in-the-Blank Round
## –Answers–

Fill-in the body of water in which the island is located.

Sunda Straight?

...Hold on...

... It's in the northeastern part of the Indian Ocean. Part of Indonesia. You're welcome.

| | | |
|---|---|---|
| 1. | Aruba | **Caribbean Sea** |
| 2. | Tonga | **Pacific Ocean** |
| 3. | Cyprus | **Mediterranean Sea** |
| 4. | Guernsey | **English Channel** |
| 5. | Bahrain | **Persian Gulf** |
| 6. | Mauritius | **Indian Ocean** |
| 7. | Lesbos | **Aegean Sea** |
| 8. | The Isle of Man | **Irish Sea** |
| 9. | Krakatoa | **Sunda Strait** |
| 10. | Three Mile Island | **Susquehanna River** |

TEAM NAME

_____

SCORE

_____

# Round Four

1. Which solo Olympic swimming race starts with the swimmer in the water?

2. In the Amazon.com logo, which two letters are connected by an arrow?

3. In the King James Bible, which country was ravaged by ten plagues?

4. In 2015, after he was convicted of domestic violence, which organization suspended driver Kurt Busch?

5. In which human organ are the myocardium, pericardium, and endocardium layers of tissue?

6. Which singer is known as the "King of Calypso"?

7. Who were the only two future presidents to have signed the Declaration of Independence?

8. Which Washington, D.C. landmark was included in the final scene of the 2001 version of *Planet of the Apes*?

9. Which town in California elected Clint Eastwood mayor in 1984?

10. Which university has won the most NCAA Division I Men's Lacrosse Championships?

**Bonus Question** Who was originally cast as the voice of Shrek?

**Q1** At the 2016 Summer Olympics in Brazil, the Olympic swimming pool was required to have lifeguards. I cannot think of a more useless job.

*What about Trivia Writer…*

No, not even my job.

# Round Four
## -Answers-

**Q8** Once again proving that the only thing you need to do to be financially successful when you remake a movie is change a small part of an iconic scene.

1.  Which solo Olympic swimming race starts with the swimmer in the water? **Backstroke**

    🖋 **Host Note** Medley relay is not a solo event.

2.  In the Amazon.com logo, which two letters are connected by an arrow? **First A and Z**

3.  In the King James Bible, which country was ravaged by ten plagues? **Egypt**

4.  In 2015, after he was convicted of domestic violence, which organization suspended driver Kurt Busch? **NASCAR**

5.  In which human organ are the myocardium, pericardium, and endocardium layers of tissue? **Heart**

6.  Which singer is known as the "King of Calypso"? **Harry Belafonte (bell-ah-fon-tay)**

7.  Who were the only two future presidents to have signed the Declaration of Independence? **John Adams and Thomas Jefferson**

    🖋 **Host Note** The Benjamin Harrison that signed is the Father of William Henry and Great Grandfather of the president Benjamin Harrison.

8.  Which Washington, D.C. landmark was included in the final scene of the 2001 version of "Planet of the Apes"? **Lincoln Memorial**

9.  Which town in California elected Clint Eastwood mayor in 1984? **Carmel-by-the-Sea**

    🖋 **Host Note** Carmel is also an acceptable answer.

10. Which university has won the most NCAA Division I Men's Lacrosse Championships? **Syracuse University**

    🖋 **Host Note** They have won ten, Johns Hopkins has nine.

    **Bonus Question** Who was originally cast as the voice of Shrek? **Chris Farley**

# Music Round

Name the song and the artist/band.

1. Do you know what's worth fighting for / When it's not worth dying for?

   _____ by _____

2. Can't stay at home, can't stay at school / Old folks say "You poor little fool"

   _____ by _____

3. I throw my hands up in the air sometimes / Saying "Ayo! Gotta let go!" / I wanna celebrate and live my life

   _____ by _____

4. Do the stanky leg (stank), do the stanky leg (stank stank) / Now break your legs / Break your legs

   _____ by _____

5. Gave you all I had and you tossed it in the trash / To give me all your love is all I ever ask

   _____ by _____

6. I need a hit / Baby, give me it / You're dangerous / I'm loving it / Too high / Can't come down / Losin' my head / Spinnin' 'round

   _____ by _____

7. Well you must be a girl with shoes like that / She said you know me well / I seen you and Little Steven and Joanna

   _____ by _____

8. Fresh new kicks...and pants / You got it like that... now you know you wanna dance

   _____ by _____

9. Make lots of noise / Kiss lots of boys / Or kiss lots of girls / If that's something you're into / When the straight and narrow

   _____ by _____

10. Ya know when that shark bites with his teeth, babe / Scarlet billows start to spread / Fancy gloves, wears old MacHeath

    _____ by _____

Theme

_____

This round is a little more violent than the others...get it... violent...it's a hint... never mind.

TEAM NAME

_____

SCORE

_____

I love Urban Dictionary. It is so helpful and speaks to me on a deeply connected level. For example, I did not know what specifically a "Stanky Leg" was. I could probably pull it, but I want to be sure.

Enter Urban Dictionary—Stanky Leg: a stupid dance, performed mostly by tools who think it's the bomb. Give it six months max before everyone realizes how moronic it is, if it's not outright forgotten because of the hype of the next throwaway dance move—the kind that will embarrass your children in twenty years. This is what we call lernin'.

**TEAM NAME**

_____

**SCORE**

_____

# Music Round
## –Answers–

Name the song and the artist/band.

1. Do you know what's worth fighting for / When it's not worth dying for? **21 Guns** by **Green Day**

2. Can't stay at home, can't stay at school / Old folks say "You poor little fool" **Cherry Bomb** by **The Runaways**

3. I throw my hands up in the air sometimes / Saying "Ayo! Gotta let go!" / I wanna celebrate and live my life **Dynamite** by **Taio Cruz**

4. Do the stanky leg (stank), do the stanky leg (stank stank) / Now break your legs/Break your legs **Watch (Whip/Nae Nae)** by **Silentó**

5. Gave you all I had and you tossed it in the trash / To give me all your love is all I ever ask **Grenade** by **Bruno Mars**

6. I need a hit / Baby, give me it / You're dangerous / I'm loving it / Too high / Can't come down / Losin' my head / Spinnin' 'round **Toxic** by **Britney Spears**

7. Well you must be a girl with shoes like that / She said you know me well / I seen you and Little Steven and Joanna **Chelsea Dagger** by **The Fratellis**

8. Fresh new kicks...and pants / You got it like that... now you know you wanna dance **U Can't Touch This** by **MC Hammer**

9. Make lots of noise/Kiss lots of boys / Or kiss lots of girls / If that's something you're into / When the straight and narrow **Follow Your Arrow** by **Kacey Musgraves**

10. Ya know when that shark bites with his teeth, babe / Scarlet billows start to spread / Fancy gloves, wears old MacHeath **Mack the Knife** by **Bobby Darin**

Theme: **Weapons**

Want more trivia?
wedontknoweither.com  dontknoweither  @wdketrivia

# Round Five

1. What number does the Roman numeral LXX represent?

2. How many atomic bombs did the U.S. drop on Japan?

3. Which primary ingredient adds bitterness to beer?

4. In a book, what is the name given to an alphabetical list of technical terms and explanations?

5. Which type of animal includes a breed called "Appaloosa"?

6. In the musical *Cabaret*, what is the name of the Berlin nightclub that is central to the story?

7. Which French philosopher is associated with the adjective "Cartesian"?

8. Which actor started his career during the silent-film era and died in 2014?

9. Which movie was the first in which Charlie Sheen played a professional baseball player?

10. In Ancient Greece, what was the function of a "rhyton"?

**Bonus Question** Which pair of literary characters are sculpted at the north end of Main St. in Hannibal, Missouri?

**Q9** Let's be honest here. If the answer was Major League would it really be a 9-point question. Use your head a little. You're supposed to be getting smarter reading this book. You are making me look bad.

# Round Five
## -Answers-

1. What number does the Roman numeral LXX represent? **Seventy (70)**

2. How many atomic bombs did the U.S. drop on Japan? **Two**

3. Which primary ingredient adds bitterness to beer? **Hops**

4. In a book, what is the name given to an alphabetical list of technical terms and explanations? **Glossary**

5. Which type of animal includes a breed called "Appaloosa"? **Horse**

6. In the musical *Cabaret*, what is the name of the Berlin nightclub that is central to the story? **The Kit Kat Klub**

7. Which French philosopher is associated with the adjective "Cartesian"? **René Descarates (day-cart)**

8. Which actor started his career during the silent film era and died in 2014? **Mickey Rooney**

9. Which movie was the first in which Charlie Sheen played a professional baseball player? *Eight Men Out*

   *Host Note* This movie was released in 1988 and Major League was released in 1989.

10. In Ancient Greece, what was the function of a "rhyton"? **A drinking vessel**

    **Bonus Question** Which pair of literary characters are sculpted at the north end of Main St. in Hannibal, Missouri? **Tom Sawyer & Huckleberry Finn**

    *Host Note* This is also the boyhood home of Mark Twain.

# GAME NINE

"Of course there's a lot of knowledge in universities: the freshmen bring a little in; the seniors don't take much away, so knowledge sort of accumulates..."

—Dr. A. Lawrence Lowell

HAT IS THE CAPITOL OF MARYLAND WHO INVENTED
HE NAME WE THE ACTIOR THAT PLAYS INDIAI
L DONT WROTE A MUSICALBASED ON THE LIFE OF WH
ATHER WHICH COMPANY MAKES THE IPAD EITHER
JUICE TO MAKE A SCREW DRIVER WHICH TWO NFL T
EW YORK HOW MANY ELEMENTS ARE ON THE PERIO
MAMBO NO 5 WHAT IS THE WESTERN MOST STAT
TES WHO WROTE THE HARRY POTTER SERIES WHAT
ACK OF THE 5 DOLLAR BILL WHAT DOES AOL STAND F
ANY MEMBERS OF THE PUSSYCAT DOLLS HOW OLD
VHICH YEAR DID HENRY FORD INVENT THE MODE
NK WAS CREATED AT THE UNIVERSITY OF FLORID/
AD ALL OF THESE QUESTIONS WHAT ARE YOU DOING V
ANY TRIVIA WRITERS DOES IT TAKE TO CHANGE A L
E BOSTON MARATHON WHAT IS THE MOST VIEWED
VHICH NETWORK HAS THE EXCLUSIVE TRIVIA TO
IOW MUCH DID A 30 SECOND NIGHT IN THE SUPERE
K IS IN THE DONE BY THE WINNER OF THE INDIANAP
IS THE GREATEST MOVIE OF ALL TIME HOW MANY EY
PLAYING CARDS WHO SHOT JR WHEN IS THE IDES (
THE NAME OF THE LEADER OF NORTH KOREA WHAT
RING MARCH MADNESS WHEN WAS THE CONSTITU TI(
NCH OF GOVERNMENT IS LEAD BY THE SUPREME C(
S DOES IT TAKE TO GET TO THE CENTER OF A TO(
HE CITY TRIVIA HEADQUARTERS WHAT DO YOU GET
V AND BLUE WHO LIVES IN THE PINEAPPLE UNDEF
HE NAME OF THE FIRST PRESIDENT OF THE UNITED
HAT WAS THE FIRST MAND MADE OBJECT TO BREAK T
HAT IS THE CAPITOL OF MARYLAND WHO INVENTED
HE NAME WE THE ACTIOR THAT PLAYS INDIA

# *Round One*

1. Which rodent shares its name with a computer device?

2. Which type of fruit is an anagram of "lemon"?

3. Which position does Harry Potter play on the Gryffindor quidditch team?

4. In the *Peanuts* cartoons, what color is Linus's security blanket?

5. Which disease of the nervous system is named after a surgeon who was born in 1755?

6. Which science fiction movie franchise included the prequel *Prometheus*?

7. Which country is the setting of the Puccini (poo-chi-knee) opera *Madame Butterfly*?

8. Which television show featured an opening credit sequence portraying relationships over time and ended with the main cast catching apples?

9. Which sport was played professionally by bank robber John Dillinger?

10. Popular as a cooked root vegetable in Europe, from which type of flower is the "Jerusalem artichoke" harvested?

**Bonus Question** The parents of which pop star run a New York restaurant called "Joanne Trattoria"?

**Q4** Are questions about the *Peanuts* comic strip still relevant with today's youth? I get complaints when I ask about 1980s cartoons, but a comic strip from the 1950s is good? Are the Peanuts more historically relevant than the *Transformers*? I guess only time will tell.

# Round One
## –Answers–

1. Which rodent shares its name with a computer device? **Mouse**

2. Which type of fruit is an anagram of "lemon"? **Melon**

3. Which position does Harry Potter play on the Gryffindor quidditch team? **Seeker**

4. In the *Peanuts* cartoons, what color is Linus's security blanket? **Blue**

5. Which disease of the nervous system is named after a surgeon who was born in 1755? **Parkinson's disease**

6. Which science fiction movie franchise included the prequel *Prometheus*? **Alien**

7. Which country is the setting of the Puccini (poo-chi-knee) opera *Madame Butterfly*? **Japan**

8. Which television show featured an opening credit sequence portraying relationships over time and ended with the main cast catching apples? **Desperate Housewives**

9. Which sport was played professionally by bank robber John Dillinger? **Baseball**

10. Popular as a cooked root vegetable in Europe, from which type of flower is the "Jerusalem artichoke" harvested? **Sunflower**

    **Bonus Question** The parents of which pop star run a New York restaurant called "Joanne Trattoria"? **Lady Gaga**

# Puzzle Round

Circle whether the book is in the top 100 challenged content or not.

1. *Captain Underpants*                Top 100 / Not

2. *The Hunger Games*                  Top 100 / Not

3. *To Kill a Mockingbird*             Top 100 / Not

4. *The Great Gatsby*                  Top 100 / Not

5. *Friday Night Lights*               Top 100 / Not

6. *The Color Purple*                  Top 100 / Not

7. *Catch-22*                          Top 100 / Not

8. *The Catcher in the Rye*            Top 100 / Not

9. *1984*                              Top 100 / Not

10. *Charlie and the*                  Top 100 / Not
    *Chocolate Factory*

"Challenged content" are books that people have requested be banned. Personally, I think it is silly to ban books. Social media, however, I am totally behind banning. Let us know what you think on Twitter @ CityTrivia.

**TEAM NAME**

_____

**SCORE**

_____

# Puzzle Round
## –Answers–

Circle whether the book is in the top 100 challenged content or not.

*Captain Underpants* is a book about how two boys accidentally hypnotize their principal into thinking he is a superhero...BAN IT! *Hunger Games* is about a rebel coup against a functional government...YEA... THAT'S COOL.

1. *Captain Underpants*    **Top 100** / Not

2. *The Hunger Games*    Top 100 / **Not**

3. *To Kill a Mockingbird*    **Top 100** / Not

4. *The Great Gatsby*    Top 100 / **Not**

5. *Friday Night Lights*    **Top 100** / Not

6. *The Color Purple*    **Top 100** / Not

7. *Catch-22*    Top 100 / **Not**

8. *The Catcher in the Rye*    **Top 100** / Not

9. *1984*    Top 100 / **Not**

10. *Charlie and the Chocolate Factory*    Top 100 / **Not**

**TEAM NAME**

**SCORE**

Want more trivia?
wedontknoweither.com   f 🐦 *dontknoweither* 📷 *@wdketrivia*

# Round Two

1. Which Pennsylvania town calls itself "Chocolate Town, U.S.A."?

2. Which cartoon series has the spinoff series *The Pebbles and Bamm-Bamm Show*?

3. According to a Belinda Carlisle song, which location "...is a place on Earth"?

4. Which system of the human body is claimed, but not scientifically proved, to be improved by the use of probiotics?

5. Which religion is the origin for the school of thought of Kabbalah (kah-bah-lah)?

6. Which gas creates the holes in Swiss cheese?

7. Which Canadian city has the largest population?

8. With 525 sacks, which quarterback holds the record for being sacked the most times in a career?

9. What was the name of Michael Jackson's first album that was not on the Motown record label?

10. In 1908, who lost the U.S. presidential election for a third time when he ran against William Howard Taft?

**Bonus Question** In which country is "Burns Night" celebrated in honor of the poet who wrote "Auld Lang Syne"?

**Q6** If there are no holes, does it count as Swiss cheese?

What are the qualifications for these kinds of things?

Who decides this?

Why have I not been consulted?

**Q8** Favre holds almost all of the records. Most times sacked. Most interceptions. In fact, at the time of his retirement, he held or shared 389 different records. Most of them are not good. Also, he lost Cameron Diaz to Ben Stiller. He probably shouldn't be in the conversation for greatest of all-time.

# Round Two
## -Answers-

1. Which Pennsylvania town calls itself "Chocolate Town, U.S.A."? **Hershey**

2. Which cartoon series has the spinoff series *The Pebbles and Bamm-Bamm Show*? ***The Flintstones***

3. According to a Belinda Carlisle song, which location "is a place on Earth"? **Heaven**

4. Which system of the human body is claimed, but not scientifically proved, to be improved by the use of probiotics? **Digestive system**

5. Which religion is the origin for the school of thought of Kabbalah (kah-bah-lah)? **Judaism**

6. Which gas creates the holes in Swiss cheese? **Carbon dioxide**

7. Which Canadian city has the largest population? **Toronto**

   ✎ **Host Note** It had a total of 2.7 million people in 2016.

8. With 525 sacks, which quarterback holds the record for being sacked the most times in a career? **Brett Favre**

9. What was the name of Michael Jackson's first album that was not on the Motown record label? ***Off the Wall***

   ✎ **Host Note** Released in 1979.

10. In 1908, who lost the U.S. presidential election for a third time when he ran against William Howard Taft? **William Jennings Bryan**

    **Bonus Question** In which country is "Burns Night" celebrated in honor of the poet who wrote "Auld Lang Syne" **Scotland**

# Picture Round

## Horror Movies: Name the Franchise

1. _____

2. _____

3. _____

4. _____

5. _____

6. _____

7. _____

8. _____

9. _____

10. _____

The funny thing about horror movies is that most of them are not scary if you watch them with the sound off. Try it. They are actually kind of funny. This is why, if you ever find yourself in a frightening situation, just cover your ears…

Boom!

Instant hilarity.

**TEAM NAME**

_____

**SCORE**

_____

I think that there is a much under-discussed plot hole in *I Know What You Did Last Summer*. I get that Ben wanted revenge against David for what he did to Ben's daughter and it makes sense that Ben is pissed he got run over, but...

*Dude, spoiler alert.*

Seriously?

**TEAM NAME**

_____

**SCORE**

_____

# Picture Round
## -Answers-
### Horror Movies: Name the Franchise

1.  **Scream**

2.  **Candy Man**

3.  **Hellraiser**

4.  **Saw**

5.  **Jeepers Creepers**

6.  **The Ring**

7.  **Sinister**

8.  **I Know What You Did Last Summer**

9.  **Leprechaun**

10.  **Critters**

Want more trivia?
wedontknoweither.com   *dontknoweither*  @wdketrivia

# Round Three

1. Traditionally, what color wine is used to make sangria?

2. How many Jokers are there in a standard deck of playing cards?

3. Which color is the "E" in the standard Google logo?

4. In which month was Julius Caesar murdered?

5. What is the term for a strip of land projecting from the main part of one U.S. state into another?

6. The measurements and proportions of what are studied in anthropometry (an-thruh-pom-eh-tree)?

7. In the movie *Field of Dreams*, in which city does Kevin Costner's character meet James Earl Jones's character?

8. Which U.S. president dedicated and opened the Empire State Building?

9. Which number does Thomas the Tank Engine have painted on his side?

10. The name of which flying vehicle is derived from the Latin phrase "to direct"?

**Bonus Question** Who was President of the United States when Barack Obama was born?

**Q7** I would love to build a baseball field in my backyard. My problem is I have no friends...and I need seventeen to play baseball. I bet you we've sold at least seventeen copies of this book.

You want to play?

**Q1** There is technically white wine sangria as well. But this is a 1-point question. You know what we are looking for.

# Round Three
## –Answers–

1. Traditionally, what color wine is used to make sangria? **Red**

2. How many Jokers are there in a standard deck of playing cards? **Two**

3. Which color is the "E" in the standard Google logo? **Red**

4. In which month was Julius Caesar murdered? **March**

   *Host Note* Specifically, it was March 15, 44 B.C.E.

5. What is the term for a strip of land projecting from the main part of one U.S. state into another? **Panhandle**

6. The measurements and proportions of what are studied in anthropometry (an-thruh-pom-eh-tree)? **Human body**

7. In the movie *Field of Dreams*, in which city does Kevin Costner's character meet James Earl Jones' character? **Boston**

8. Which U.S. president dedicated and opened the Empire State Building? **Herbert Hoover**

   *Host Note* It was on May 1, 1931—he turned on the lights from Washington, D.C.

9. Which number does Thomas the Tank Engine have painted on his side? **One**

10. The name of which flying vehicle is derived from the Latin for "to direct"? **Dirigible**

    **Bonus Question** Who was President of the United States when Barack Obama was born? **John F. Kennedy**

    *Host Note* Obama was born on August 4, 1961 and JFK took office on January 20, 1961.

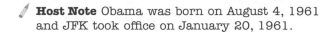

# Fill-in-the-Blank Round

Fill-in the movie in which the Oscar-winning song appears.

1. Chim Chim Cher-ee (1964)

   _____

2. Take My Breath Away (1986)

   _____

3. A Whole New World (1992)

   _____

4. If I Didn't Have You (2001)

   _____

5. Lose Yourself (2002)

   _____

6. Jai Ho (2008)

   _____

7. We Belong Together (2010)

   _____

8. Let it Go (2013)

   _____

9. Glory (2014)

   _____

10. Into the West (2003)

   _____

"Let It Go" is the most pervasive song of all-time. I have a daughter. I am intimately aware of how that song burrows into your head and stakes its claim. I unknowingly sing it so much that they will put "The cold never bothered him anyway" on my tombstone. Also, I plan to die summiting Everest. So it will actually all work out in the end.

**TEAM NAME**

_____

**SCORE**

_____

# Fill-in-the-Blank Round
## -Answers-

Fill-in the movie in which the Oscar-winning song appears.

Apparently, all Disney needs to do is make a movie and put a song in it and they win an Oscar. Seem a little like cheating if you ask me.

1. Chim Chim Cher-ee (1964)     *Mary Poppins*

2. Take My Breath Away (1986)     *Top Gun*

3. A Whole New World (1992)     *Aladdin*

4. If I Didn't Have You (2001)     *Monsters, Inc.*

5. Lose Yourself (2002)     *8 Mile*

6. Jai Ho (2008)     *Slumdog Millionaire*

7. We Belong Together (2010)     *Toy Story 3*

8. Let it Go (2013)     *Frozen*

9. Glory (2014)     *Selma*

10. Into the West (2003)     *Lord of the Rings*

**TEAM NAME**

_____

**SCORE**

_____

# Round Four

1. In the game tic-tac-toe, how many symbols in a row are needed to win?

2. Which is the only chemical element that has the same exact name as a planet?

3. In the movie *The Big Lebowski*, who played "The Dude"?

4. What is the term for a male honeybee?

5. Which pandemic killed millions of people during and after World War I?

6. Which is the only U.S. city to have hosted the Summer Olympics twice?

7. Which military title is held by the current international leader of the Salvation Army?

8. The name of which small French cake means "little oven"?

9. Which is the longest vein in the human body?

10. How many chemical elements on the periodic table are defined by a single-letter symbol?

    **Bonus Question** Who is aboard an aircraft with the call sign "Shepherd One"?

**Q10** There are twenty-six letters in the alphabet, it's probably less than that.

**Q1** If you play the right way, it is impossible to lose a game of tic-tac-toe. So why do you lose? I'll give you a hint: if you go first, start in the corner.

# Round Four
## -Answers-

1. In the game tic-tac-toe, how many symbols in a row are needed to win? **Three (3)**

2. Which is the only chemical element that has the same exact name as a planet? **Mercury**

   🖉 **Host Note** Neptunium and Uranium are derivations of planet names.

3. In the movie *The Big Lebowski*, who played "The Dude"? **Jeff Bridges**

4. What is the term for a male honeybee? **Drones**

5. Which pandemic killed millions of people during and after World War I? **Spanish flu (La Grippe)**

6. Which is the only U.S. city to have hosted the Summer Olympics twice? **Los Angeles**

   🖉 **Host Note** This occurred in 1932 and 1984. We are also selected to host the 2028 Summer Olympics.

7. Which military title is held by the current international leader of the Salvation Army? **General**

8. The name of which small French cake means "little oven"? **Petit four (petty-fore)**

9. Which is the longest vein in the human body? **Great Saphenous**

10. How many chemical elements on the periodic table are defined by a single-letter symbol? **Fourteen (14)**

    **Bonus Question** Who is aboard an aircraft with the call sign "Shepherd One"? **Pope (Bishop of Rome)**

# Music Round

Name the song and the artist/band.

1. Look over there! (Where?) / There's a lady that I used to know / She's married now, or engaged, or something, so I am told

   _____ by _____

2. I've been awake for a while now / You've got me feelin' like a child now / Every time I see your bubbly face / I get the tingles in a silly place

   _____ by _____

3. We both got fired on, exactly, the same day / Well, we'll float on, good news is on the way

   _____ by _____

4. Whenever we meet, we ain't gonna get no sleep / When I get to be together with you / It's fait accompli

   _____ by _____

5. And I lift my hands and pray / To be only yours I pray / To be only yours I know now you're my only hope

   _____ by _____

6. I'll make ya bump bump wiggle and shake your rump / 'Cause I'll be kicking the flavor that makes you wanna jump

   _____ by _____

7. I've got another confession to make / I'm your fool / Everyone's got their chains to break / Holdin' you

   _____ by _____

8. Hot in the kitchen like a thousand degrees / That's how I'm feeling when you're next to me

   _____ by _____

9. I've seen you on the beach and I've seen you on TV / Two of a billion stars it means so much to me

   _____ by _____

10. You are my fire / The one desire / Believe when I say / I want it that way

    _____ by _____

Theme

_____

I don't think there is enough foreign language in music today.

_"Despacito" is the #1 ranked video on YouTube with over 5 billion views._

Oh...

...never mind.

**TEAM NAME**

_____

**SCORE**

_____

# Music Round
## —Answers—

Name the song and the artist/band.

Alliterative Artists is a fun theme. It is also alliterative itself. Themeception.

1. Look over there! (Where?) / There's a lady that I used to know / She's married now, or engaged, or something, so I am told
**Is She Really Going Out with Him?** by **Joe Jackson**

2. I've been awake for a while now / You've got me feelin' like a child now / Every time I see your bubbly face / I get the tingles in a silly place
**Bubbly** by **Colbie Caillat**

3. We both got fired on, exactly, the same day / Well, we'll float on, good news is on the way
**Float On** by **Modest Mouse**

4. Whenever we meet, we ain't gonna get no sleep / When I get to be together with you / It's fait accompli
**No Sleep** by **Janet Jackson**

5. And I lift my hands and pray / To be only yours I pray / To be only yours I know now you're my only hope
**Only Hope** by **Mandy Moore**

6. I'll make ya bump bump wiggle and shake your rump / 'Cause I'll be kicking the flavor that makes you wanna jump
**Jump** by **Kris Kross**

7. I've got another confession to make / I'm your fool / Everyone's got their chains to break / Holdin' you
**Best of You** by **Foo Fighters**

8. Hot in the kitchen like a thousand degrees / That's how I'm feeling when you're next to me
**Burnin' Up** by **Jessie J**

9. I've seen you on the beach and I've seen you on TV / Two of a billion stars it means so much to me
**Rio** by **Duran Duran**

10. You are my fire / The one desire / Believe when I say / I want it that way
**I Want It That Way** by **Backstreet Boys**

Theme: **Alliterative Artists**

**TEAM NAME**

_____

**SCORE**

_____

# Round Five

1. Which year came directly after 10 B.C.E.?

2. Which Chinese landmark has been measured at over 13,000 miles in total length?

3. Which type of fruit includes the varieties Rainier and Bing?

4. From 1935–1972, which organization was led by J. Edgar Hoover?

5. After which player is the U.S. Tennis Association's National Tennis Center named?

6. The name of which Egyptian goddess is the Greek form of an ancient Egyptian word for "throne"?

7. In the musical *Les Misérables*, which character performs the song "I Dreamed a Dream"?

8. Which term for a type of number is Latin for "whole" or "intact"?

9. Operating as a state park, in which U.S. state is the only active diamond mine?

10. Who is the only NFL (National Football League) coach to win three Super Bowls with three different quarterbacks?

**Bonus Question** At his own request, the autobiography of which writer was not published in its entirety until 2010, one hundred years after his death?

**Q3** Trivia Night Hint: Fruits have a lot of varieties. Take a few of the big-name fruits: apples, oranges, bananas, pears, and memorize a few of their biggest varieties. It will help. I promise.

**Q10** Since Gibbs left the first time, the Redskins have only won two playoff games. We should probably get him back.

*We did, it didn't work.* Whelp, I'm out of ideas then.

# Round Five
## -Answers-

1. Which year came directly after 10 B.C.E.? **9 B.C.E.**

2. Which Chinese landmark has been measured at over 13,000 miles in total length? **The Great Wall of China**

3. Which type of fruit includes the varieties Rainier and Bing? **Cherry**

4. From 1935–1972, which organization was led by J. Edgar Hoover? **Federal Bureau of Investigation (FBI)**

5. After which player is the U.S. Tennis Association's National Tennis Center named? **Billie Jean King**

   ✎ **Host Note** The full name of the center is USTA Billie Jean King National Tennis Center.

6. The name of which Egyptian goddess is the Greek form of an ancient Egyptian word for "throne"? **Isis**

7. In the musical *Les Misérables,* which character performs the song "I Dreamed a Dream"? **Fantine (fawn-tine)**

8. Which term for a type of number is Latin for "whole" or "intact"? **Integer**

9. Operating as a state park, in which U.S. state is the only active diamond mine? **Arkansas**

   ✎ **Host Note** Visitors can pay a fee and keep what they find.

10. Who is the only NFL (National Football League) coach to win three Super Bowls with three different quarterbacks? **Joe Gibbs**

    ✎ **Host Note** With the Washington Redskins.

    **Bonus Question** At his own request, the autobiography of which writer was not published in its entirety until 2010, one hundred years after his death? **Mark Twain**

# GAME
# TEN

"So you see! There's no end to the things you might know,
depending how far beyond zebra you go."

—Dr. Seuss

HAT IS THE CAPITOL OF MARYLAND WHO INVENTE

THE NAME WE THE ACTIOR THAT PLAYS INDIA

L DONT WROTE A MUSICALBASED ON THE LIFE OF W

FATHER WHICH COMPANY MAKES THE IPAD EITHER

JUICE TO MAKE A SCREW DRIVER WHICH TWO NFL

EW YORK HOW MANY ELEMENTS ARE ON THE PERIO

MAMBO NO 5 WHAT IS THE WESTERN MOST STA

ATES WHO WROTE THE HARRY POTTER SERIES WHAT

BACK OF THE 5 DOLLAR BILL WHAT DOES AOL STAND

MANY MEMBERS OF THE PUSSYCAT DOLLS HOW OLI

WHICH YEAR DID HENRY FORD INVENT THE MODE

INK WAS CREATED AT THE UNIVERSITY OF FLORID

AD ALL OF THESE QUESTIONS WHAT ARE YOU DOING

MANY TRIVIA WRITERS DOES IT TAKE TO CHANGE A

HE BOSTON MARATHON WHAT IS THE MOST VIEWEI

WHICH NETWORK HAS THE EXCLUSIVE TRIVIA TO

HOW MUCH DID A 30 SECOND NIGHT IN THE SUPERI

K IS IN THE DONE BY THE WINNER OF THE INDIANAF

IS THE GREATEST MOVIE OF ALL TIME HOW MANY EY

PLAYING CARDS WHO SHOT JR WHEN IS THE IDES

THE NAME OF THE LEADER OF NORTH KOREA WHA

RING MARCH MADNESS WHEN WAS THE CONSTITU TI

NCH OF GOVERNMENT IS LEAD BY THE SUPREME C

S DOES IT TAKE TO GET TO THE CENTER OF A TO

HE CITY TRIVIA HEADQUARTERS WHAT DO YOU GET

W AND BLUE WHO LIVES IN THE PINEAPPLE UNDE

THE NAME OF THE FIRST PRESIDENT OF THE UNITED

HAT WAS THE FIRST MAND MADE OBJECT TO BREAK

HAT IS THE CAPITOL OF MARYLAND WHO INVENTE

HE NAME WE THE ACTIOR THAT PLAYS INDIA

# Round One

1.  What is the name of the MLB championship series?

2.  Which family of musical instruments includes the tuba?

3.  The archenemy of which fictional detective is Professor Moriarty?

4.  Which term describes words with the same spelling and pronunciation, but different meanings?

5.  Which precious metal has the atomic number 79?

6.  Who was the original subject of the Elton John song "Candle in the Wind"?

7.  Who was both the twenty-second and twenty-fourth U.S. president?

8.  What is the common name for a tree in the genus Quercus (kwer-kuss)?

9.  In which part of a living cell are functions for cell expansion, growth, and replication carried out?

10. In the 2001 movie *Moulin Rouge*, which pop singer played the Green Fairy?

    **Bonus Question** In Scotland, which annual holiday is "Hogmanay" (hog-ma-nay)?

**Q6** The remake of the song was about Princess Diana. That version is the second bestselling song of all time. I wish I could take something I have already produced and repackage it for more profit.

That's an inside joke.

If you don't get it, you're not on the inside.

**Q3** Professor Moriarty is one of the great characters in literature. A match for the greatest detective in the world AND Data from Star Trek AND Robert Downey Jr.

That last one should show you how great he really is.

# Round One
## -Answers-

1. What is the name of the MLB championship series? **World Series**

2. Which family of musical instruments includes the tuba? **Brass**

3. The archenemy of which fictional detective is Professor Moriarty? **Sherlock Holmes**

4. Which term describes words with the same spelling and pronunciation, but different meanings? **Homonym**

5. Which precious metal has the atomic number 79? **Gold**

6. Who was the original subject of the Elton John song "Candle in the Wind"? **Marilyn Monroe (Norma Jeane)**

7. Who was both the twenty-second and twenty-fourth U.S. president? **Grover Cleveland**

8. What is the common name for a tree in the genus Quercus (kwer-kuss)? **Oak**

9. In which part of a living cell are functions for cell expansion, growth, and replication carried out? **Cytoplasm**

10. In the 2001 movie *Moulin Rouge*, which pop singer played the Green Fairy? **Kylie Minogue (min-oh)**

**Bonus Question** In Scotland, which annual holiday is "Hogmanay" (hog-ma-nay)? **New Year's Eve or "Last Day of the Year"**

# Puzzle Round

Provide an English word that contains the given fragment.

1. oribu _____

2. tatis _____

3. rigu _____

4. iang _____

5. poch _____

6. hibia _____

7. talou _____

8. vv _____

9. ghfa _____

10. perl _____

Word fragments are tough pull for a puzzle round. You never know how many letters come before or after. Do *any* letters come before? Could these letters be the beginning or the end or a word?

You're on your own... I am awful at this.

**TEAM NAME**

_____

**SCORE**

_____

There were two answers for VV. I didn't get either of them. Did you?

# Puzzle Round
## -Answers-

Provide an English word that contains the given fragment.

1. oribu      **Moribund**

2. tatis      **Statistics**

3. rigu      **Intrigue**

4. iang      **Triangle**

5. poch      **Epoch**

6. hibia      **Amphibian**

7. talou      **Cantaloupe**

8. vv      **Revved or Savvy**

9. ghfa      **Thoroughfare**

10. perl      **Superlative**

**TEAM NAME**

_____

**SCORE**

_____

# Round Two

1.  Until 1998, which pop group included Geri Halliwell?

2.  In the *Star Trek* franchise, on which planet was Spock born?

**Q1** When Geri left I was devastated. This is not a joke. Total devastation.

3.  In the music term "Prog Rock," what is "prog" short for?

4.  The name of which Mexican snack food translates roughly to "little cheese thing"?

5.  In which city is the original Taj Mahal located?

6.  Which *Star Wars* character was played by Peter Mayhew?

7.  How many symphonies did Beethoven complete?

8.  In World War II, what was the codename for the 1941 Axis attack on the Soviet Union?

9.  What is the nationality of the professional boxers Vitali and Wladmir Klitschko?

10. Which symbol is in the center of Morocco's national flag?

**Bonus Question** Which material is patented under the name "Wholly aromatic carbocyclic polycarbonamide fiber having orientation of less than about 45 degrees"?

**Q7** Bonus Trivia Fact: Beethoven's unfinished symphony was his tenth. That is probably obvious now, but here we are.

# Round Two
## –Answers–

1. Until 1998, which pop group included Geri Halliwell? **Spice Girls**

2. In the *Star Trek* franchise, on which planet was Spock born? **Vulcan**

3. In the music term "Prog Rock," what is "prog" short for? **Progressive**

4. The name of which Mexican snack food translates roughly to "little cheese thing"? **Quesadilla**

5. In which city is the original Taj Mahal located? **Agra, India**

6. Which Star Wars character was played by Peter Mayhew? **Chewbacca**

7. How many symphonies did Beethoven complete? **Nine (9)**

8. In World War II, what was the codename for the 1941 Axis attack on the Soviet Union? **Operation Barbarossa**

9. What is the nationality of the professional boxers Vitali and Wladmir Klitschko? **Ukrainian**

   *Host Note* Born in the formerly named U.S.S.R.

10. Which symbol is in the center of Morocco's national flag? **Star**

    *Host Note* Specifically a five-pointed star or pentagram.

    **Bonus Question** Which material is patented under the name "Wholly aromatic carbocyclic polycarbonamide fiber having orientation of less than about 45 degrees"? **Kevlar**

# Picture Round

## Currency: Name the Country

1. _____

2. _____

3. _____

4. _____

5. _____

6. _____

7. _____

8. _____

9. _____

10. _____

Trivia Tip: If you can afford it, travel. As much and as far as you can. You will learn more from a week in a new place than from a month of studying. Perspective changes everything.

**TEAM NAME**

_____

**SCORE**

_____

How bad does your economy have to be in order to legitimately print an official one hundred trillion dollar bill? You could wallpaper your house with money and it would be a better use.

# Picture Round
## -Answers-

Currency: Name the Country

1. **Japan (Yen)**

2. **Mexico (Peso)**

3. **Costa Rica (Colon)**

4. **Zimbabwe (Dollar)**

5. **Norway (Kroner)**

6. **Mongolia (Togrog)**

7. **China (Yuan)**

8. **Israel (New Shekel)**

9. **Jamaica (Dollar)**

10. **South Africa (Rand)**

**TEAM NAME**

**SCORE**

# Round Three

1.  In the acronym "HDTV," what does "HD" stand for?

2.  According to the proverb, absence makes what grow fonder?

3.  In 1988, which scientist wrote the book *A Brief History of Time*?

4.  Which Pennsylvania city is the setting for the U.S. version of the television series *The Office*?

5.  What is measured by the Beaufort Scale?

6.  As of 2018, which NFL (National Football League) quarterback holds the record for most passing touchdowns in a single season?

7.  Which Shakespearean play is primarily set in "Elsinore Castle"?

8.  In 1999, which country gave sovereignty of Macau back to China?

9.  The feminine name "Melissa" is derived from the Greek word for which insect?

10. Which acid was once referred to as "oil of vitriol"?

**Bonus Question** Helping to modernize the sport in the 1800s, which sport is U.S. ballet dancer Jackson Haines considered "the Father of"?

**Q1** We are now producing TVs that have pictures in 8K. It's a reasonable $21,000 from Samsung. The human eye, in perfect condition, can differentiate up to 28K pictures at the appropriate distance and size. I guess we still have a few more years of new TVs ahead of us.

**Q7** Synopsis for *Hamlet*: No one is honest with anyone and everyone dies. That's actually the summary for most Shakespeare plays. Actually, that's the summary for most entertainment.

# Round Three
## –Answers–

1. In the acronym "HDTV," what does "HD" stand for? **High Definition**

2. According to the proverb, absence makes what grow fonder? **Heart**

3. In 1988, which scientist wrote the book *A Brief History of Time*? **Stephen Hawking**

4. Which Pennsylvania city is the setting for the U.S. version of the television series *The Office*? **Scranton**

5. What is measured by the Beaufort Scale? **Wind speed**

6. As of 2018, which NFL (National Football League) quarterback holds the record for most passing touchdowns in a single season? **Peyton Manning**

   **Host Note** With 55 in 2013.

7. Which Shakespearean play is primarily set in "Elsinore Castle"? *Hamlet*

8. In 1999, which country gave sovereignty of Macau back to China? **Portugal**

9. The feminine name "Melissa" is derived from the Greek word for which insect? **Honeybee**

10. Which acid was once referred to as "oil of vitriol"? **Sulfuric acid**

    **Bonus Question** Helping to modernize the sport in the 1800s, which sport is U.S. ballet dancer Jackson Haines considered the "father" of? **Figure skating**

# Fill-in-the-Blank Round

Fill-in the name of the character played by both actors.

1. Iam Holm, Martin Freeman

   _____

2. Josh Brolin, Tommy Lee Jones

   _____

3. Rob Lowe, Robert Wagner

   _____

4. River Phoenix, Harrison Ford

   _____

5. Ian McKellen, Michael Fassbender

   _____

6. Jack Nicholson, Heath Ledger

   _____

7. Chris Evans, Michael B. Jordan

   _____

8. Anthony Hopkins, Brian Cox

   _____

9. Richard Harris, Michael Gambon

   _____

10. Billy Dee Williams, Tommy Lee Jones

   _____

Chris Evans may have played two super heroes, but Ryan Reynolds has played more than six, including Deadpool twice. Even more impressive is that none of them are any good. Except maybe Deadpool. *Wolverine Origins* was a great film. See what I did there, you thought I was going one way and I went the other. Comedy.

**TEAM NAME**

_____

**SCORE**

_____

# Fill-in-the-Blank Round
## –Answers–

Fill-in the name of the character played by both actors.

OK, debate time. Best Jokers. Nicholson? Ledger? Nope. Mark Hamill. Number one seed by far.

*But he played Luke Skywalker, not the Joker.*

Oh ye of little faith. Mark Hamill was the voice of the Joker in *Batman the Animated Series*. Best Joker ever. Watch it.

1. Iam Holm, Martin Freeman — **Bilbo Baggins**

2. Josh Brolin, Tommy Lee Jones — **Agent K**

3. Rob Lowe, Robert Wagner — **Number Two**

    **Host Note** In the film *Austin Powers*.

4. River Phoenix, Harrison Ford — **Indiana Jones**

5. Ian McKellen, Michael Fassbender — **Magneto**

6. Jack Nicholson, Heath Ledger — **The Joker**

7. Chris Evans, Michael B. Jordan — **Johnny Storm/ Human Torch**

8. Anthony Hopkins, Brian Cox — **Hannibal Lecter**

9. Richard Harris, Michael Gambon — **Albus Dumbledore**

10. Billy Dee Williams, Tommy Lee Jones — **Harvey Dent**

    **Host Note** In the film *Batman Forever*.

**TEAM NAME**

**SCORE**

# *Round Four*

1. Which chemical element has the symbol "O"?

2. How many railroads are on a standard "Monopoly" board?

**Q2** Technically, Short Line is owned by a bus company, but for the purposes of this question let's not get technical.

3. Which human organ is primarily affected by emphysema (emm-fa-zee-ma)?

4. In Greek mythology, which river forms the boundary between Earth and the Underworld?

5. The name of which religious festival is derived from the Latin phrase "a removal of meat"?

6. Every July, which Canadian city hosts the "Just for Laughs Comedy Festival"?

7. In 1900, which company published its first "guide" and in 1926 began rating restaurants with stars?

8. In which sport do players compete for the "Thomas Cup"?

9. Which country is the origin of the comedy duo "Flight of Conchords"?

10. In the cartoon series *Doug*, what was the full name of Doug's female love interest?

**Bonus Question** Which 1996 movie was written by Michael Crichton and starred Helen Hunt and Bill Paxton?

**Q5** Given the lack of clothing and glamorous headdresses, Carnival seems to have come a long way from no meat.

# Round Four
## –Answers–

1. Which chemical element has the symbol "O"? **Oxygen**

2. How many railroads are on a standard Monopoly board? **Four (4)**

3. Which human organ is primarily affected by emphysema (emm-fa-zee-ma)? **Lung**

4. In Greek mythology, which river forms the boundary between Earth and the Underworld? **Styx**

5. The name of which religious festival is derived from the Latin phrase "a removal of meat"? **Carnival**

6. Every July, which Canadian city hosts the "Just for Laughs Comedy Festival"? **Montréal**

7. In 1900, which company published its first "guide" and in 1926 began rating restaurants with stars? **Michelin**

   🖉 **Host Note** Yes, it is published by the tire company. It began as a guide to get people to drive more and to different places.

8. In which sport do players compete for the "Thomas Cup"? **Badminton**

9. Which country is the origin of the comedy duo "Flight of Conchords"? **New Zealand**

10. In the cartoon series *Doug*, what was the full name of Doug's female love interest? **Patty Mayonnaise**

    **Bonus Question** Which 1996 movie was written by Michael Crichton and starred Helen Hunt and Bill Paxton? **Twister**

# Music Round

Name the song and the artist/band.

1. I saw a werewolf with a Chinese menu in his hand /
   Walking through the streets of Soho in the rain

   _____ by _____

2. What would I do without your smart mouth /
   Drawing me in, and you kicking me out

   _____ by _____

3. But I'd play with fire to break the ice / And I'd play
   with a nuclear device/Is it something I'll regret?

   _____ by _____

4. I might have to wait/I'll never give up / I guess it's
   half timing and the other half's luck

   _____ by _____

5. We fly high, no lie, you know this (Ballin'!) / Foreign
   rides, outside, it's like showbiz (We in the building)

   _____ by _____

6. Show me round your fruit cakes / 'Cause I will be
   your honey bee/Open up your fruit cakes / Where
   the fruit is as sweet as can be

   _____ by _____

7. So baby take my hand, you'll be all right / Surrender
   all your dreams to me tonight

   _____ by _____

8. It doesn't matter what I say / So long as I sing with
   inflection / That makes you feel I'll convey / Some
   inner truth or vast reflection

   _____ by _____

9. We drinking Santana champ, 'cause it's so
   crisp (crisp) / I got my swim trunks, and my
   flippie-floppies

   _____ by _____

10. Wake up in the morning feeling like P. Diddy (Hey,
    what up girl?) / Grab my glasses, I'm out the door,
    I'm gonna hit this city (Let's go)

    _____ by _____

Theme

_____

Some themes are easy. Some are creative. Some are hard. This round is both of the latter. Good luck. Seriously. This one is really creative.

TEAM NAME

_____

SCORE

_____

# Music Round
## –Answers–

Name the song and the artist/band.

I was at college with John Legend. He was John Stephens then. He is one of those people who is really easy to hate. Unbelievable talent, incredibly smart, and honestly one of the nicest people I've ever met.

Bastard.

1. I saw a werewolf with a Chinese menu in his hand / Walking through the streets of Soho in the rain **Werewolves of London** by **Warren Zevon**

2. What would I do without your smart mouth / Drawing me in, and you kicking me out **All of Me** by **John Legend**

3. But I'd play with fire to break the ice / And I'd play with a nuclear device/Is it something I'll regret? **Wendy Clear** by **Blink-182**

4. I might have to wait/I'll never give up /I guess it's half timing and the other half's luck **Haven't Met You Yet** by **Michael Bublé**

5. We fly high, no lie, you know this (Ballin'!) / Foreign rides, outside, it's like showbiz (We in the building) **We Fly High** by **Jim Jones**

6. Show me round your fruit cakes / 'Cause I will be your honey bee / Open up your fruit cakes / Where the fruit is as sweet as can be **Sledgehammer** by **Peter Gabriel**

7. So baby take my hand, you'll be all right /Surrender all your dreams to me tonight **Shadows of the Night** by **Pat Benatar**

8. It doesn't matter what I say / So long as I sing with inflection / That makes you feel I'll convey / Some inner truth or vast reflection **Hook** by **Blues Traveler**

9. We drinking Santana champ, 'cause it's so crisp (crisp) / I got my swim trunks, and my flippie-floppies **I'm On a Boat** by **The Lonely Island**

10. Wake up in the morning feeling like P Diddy (Hey, what up girl?)/Grab my glasses, I'm out the door, I'm gonna hit this city (Let's go) **Tik Tok** by **Ke$ha**

Theme: **Peter Pan**

**TEAM NAME**

_____

**SCORE**

_____

# Round Five

1. The postal abbreviation for which U.S. state is "O.K."?

2. In law, which Latin phrase translates to "you shall have the body"?

Postal abbreviations are huge, easy questions for trivia night. Fifty states, fifty abbreviations. Study up.

3. Which mobile phone company is headquartered in Espoo, Finland?

4. What is the common name of the garden flower Helianthus (hell-ee-ann-thus)?

5. For which fictional television town does "Diamond" Joe Quimby serve as the mayor?

6. Played by Clint Eastwood, which classic car is the prize possession of the movie character Walt Kowalski?

7. Which type of fruit is used to make Calvados brandy?

8. In the children's stories, from which country has Paddington Bear arrived when he is found in the London Train Station?

9. What is primarily eaten by a graminivorous (gram-in-iv-or-us) animal?

10. In classical architecture, what term refers to a draped female figure used instead of a column as support?

**Bonus Question** How many Winter Olympics have been hosted by the United States?

Nokia being a phone company is accurate. But depending on how their phones are used, they could also be a concrete company, a weapons manufacturer, or a gym equipment producer. Seriously, I still have my Nokia 6110. If I plug it in, it still works. It is amazing.

# Round Five
## -Answers-

1. The postal abbreviation for which U.S. state is "O.K."? **Oklahoma**

2. In law, which Latin phrase translates to "you shall have the body"? **Habeas corpus**

3. Which mobile phone company is headquartered in Espoo, Finland? **Nokia**

4. What is the common name of the garden flower Helianthus (hell-ee-ann-thus)? **Sunflower**

5. For which fictional television town does "Diamond" Joe Quimby serve as the mayor? **Springfield**

   *Host Note* On *The Simpsons*.

6. Played by Clint Eastwood, which classic car is the prize possession of the movie character Walt Kowalski? **Ford Gran Torino**

   *Host Note* In the movie of the same name.

7. Which type of fruit is used to make Calvados brandy? **Apples**

8. In the children's stories, from which country has Paddington Bear arrived when he is found in the London Train Station? **Peru**

9. What is primarily eaten by a graminivorous (gram-in-iv-or-us) animal? **Grass (or grass seeds)**

10. In classical architecture, what term refers to a draped female figure used instead of a column as support? **Caryatid (carry-at-id)**

    **Bonus Question** How many Winter Olympics have been hosted by the United States? **Four (4)**

# Closing Words

So, that is the book. Please remember to tip your bartenders and servers. Seriously though, if you have made it this far you have accomplished at least a few things.

First, you should be considerably more intelligent. It is impossible to retain nothing from this book, something must have gotten stuck in the gelatinous mass on top of your shoulders. Congrats, you can now annoy people with your random knowledge just like the rest of us.

Second, if you have used this book to run a trivia night of your own, you'll find yourself facing a small problem. You are now out of trivia nights. So what do you do now? I have two great options for you. If it is far enough into the future, you can simply pick up Volume II of *We Don't Know Either*. If enough time hasn't passed, or if you are sick of copying pages and stapling them together, you can simply visit iHeartCityTrivia.com. We will produce a packet of trivia so professional you will swoon and mail it directly to your door.

Regardless, Thanks for playing. We will see you next time.

# Acknowledgements

None of this book would have been possible without the help of:

Jared Campbell

Lindsey Bitler

David Walker

Michael Causey

Nick Hardt

Drea Barricklow

Angela Olson

And the many hosts that bring trivia to life in the neighborhood bars and restaurants every week.

Also, my parents Glenn and Kay, and my wife Sarah. Without your love, support, and advice none of this would exist.

What? This may be my only book, I had to get everyone in there, didn't I?

# About the Author

## Nick Groves

Nick Groves is the founder and CEO of City Trivia, the parent company of District Trivia in Washington, D.C.; Bridgetown Trivia in Portland, OR; Old Line Trivia in Baltimore, MD; and Patriot Trivia in Boston, MA. Since 2009, he and his staff have hosted thousands of trivia nights in hundreds of bars in dozens of states and five countries on four continents.

Nick co-hosts the We Don't Know Either podcast and has been a guest on NBC Sports Washington, CBS Radio, the Trivial Warfare podcast, and D.C. television news shows. Washington-area sports fans know him as the host of "Minute to Win It," where players can prove their trivia skills outside of the pub and on TV. This is his debut book.

Nick and his wife, Sarah, are the parents of two young children, Asher and Charlotte, and reside in Potomac, MD, with their two cats. He is grateful for his hardworking staff, without whom this book would not have been possible, especially Drea Barricklow, Lindsey Bitler, Jared Campbell, Michael Causey, Nick Hardt, Angela Olson, Dave Walker, and the many hosts who bring trivia to life in neighborhood bars and restaurants every week.

## City Trivia

City Trivia is your neighborhood pub trivia done right. The best hosts, the best format, and the best prizes combine so that you have the best time possible. Why are we the best?

Reason 1: We are trivia done by players for players. Trivia is about having fun with your friends and proving to them you know more random things than they do...also proving it to everyone else in the room.

Reason 2: Format is important. We have five rounds of trivia and four bonus rounds with a variety of questions. The pace is fast, the question topics are varied, and the host is entertaining.

Reason 3: City Trivia is about developing a community of people who like playing trivia. We are smart and so are our players. It is not just

City Trivia that makes this book special...it is the entire City Trivia community—the bars and restaurants that hire us, the players who show up every week all season long, the friends, family, and co-workers who enjoy dinner, drinks, and competing for prizes. Buy our book, laugh at our host, argue about the answers... Join us!

Learn more about City Trivia at iHeartCityTrivia.com, and listen to our popular podcast *We Don't Know Either* on Podomatic or at WeDontKnowEither.com.